Teaching 14–19

Teaching 14–19:
A Handbook

John Bostock and Jane Wood

Mc Graw Hill Open University Press

Open University Press
McGraw-Hill Education
McGraw-Hill House
Shoppenhangers Road
Maidenhead
Berkshire
England
SL6 2QL

email: enquiries@openup.co.uk
world wide web: www.openup.co.uk

and
Two Penn Plaza, New York, NY 10121-2289, USA

First published 2012

A catalogue record of this book is available from the British Library

ISBN-13: 978-0-33-524191-0 (pb) 978-0-33-524190-3 (hb)
ISBN-10: 033524191-3 (pb) 033524190-5
e-ISBN: 9780335241927

Library of Congress Cataloging-in-Publication Data
CIP data applied for

Typeset by Aptara Inc., India
Printed in the UK by Bell and Bain Ltd, Glasgow.

Fictitious names of companies, products, people, characters and/or data that may be used herein (in case studies or in examples) are not intended to represent any real individual, company, product or event.

MIX
Paper from
responsible sources
FSC® C007785

The *McGraw-Hill* Companies

Contents

This book is produced in memory of our grandparents who influenced us and believed in us:

John and Elizabeth Reay
James and Frances Ellen Bostock
Richard and Eva Griffiths
Alan and Evelyn Wright
Lawrence Ryan

We also dedicate this book to our parents for all their love, support and encouragement:

James and Teresa Bostock
David and Heather Ryan

Acknowledgements

We would like to thank David Ryan and Paul Hutchinson for all their help and support in editing and formatting this book.

We would also like to thank the following colleagues for their contributions: Myrtle Chadderton; Andrew George; Karen Greig; Alison Harrison; Genevieve Parkes; Sandra Parr; Lorraine Roberts; Sally Ryan and Chris Taylor.

Introduction

For a long time the age of 14 has been a significant time of transformation in the lives of young people. In the current education system they are asked to take their 'options' and to choose the subjects they want to study for the rest of their education. This has developed from a narrow choice of academic subjects to a much wider range of vocational and academic subjects, often delivered in partnership with local colleges. This is a great step forward and an essential way of engaging young people in education at a very difficult time of their lives.

However, staff in colleges have not been well prepared for these changes. Often they have had no specific training in teaching these younger learners and are completely unaware of the increased safeguarding and support issues involved. The aim of this book is to provide some very practical and clear guidance on how to teach these younger learners. We focus extensively on how to manage behaviour as this is the most frequently raised issue among tutors/practitioners. We also give clear tips and techniques for you to try in the classroom and supplement this by drawing on real-life case studies from our own experience or that of our colleagues. It is important to understand how students learn so the theory that supports this as well as the role of assessment in this process is covered too.

This book is based squarely on our own experiences in the sector together with our own research and has its foundation in real-life practical situations. We anticipate that the book will be a valuable source of reference and a helpful guide to support trainee and newly qualified tutors practitioners, whether in schools or colleges, to teach 14–19-year-old learners with confidence and pride.

With the real-life case studies, suggested reading and practical tasks, the chapters provide an insightful journey through the world of 14–19 education. It has been a collaboration between colleagues and has been influenced every step of the way by the experiences of the many trainee teachers we teach, observe, tutor and support in our jobs as senior lecturers at Edge Hill University.

We are only ever as good as the students we teach and their success is our success and their failure is our responsibility. We are very lucky to have the opportunity to be part of these young people's lives at such an important time and this responsibility must be taken seriously. They deserve the very best opportunity to embrace learning and to proceed onwards to become lifelong learners and active citizens in our society.

What an opportunity – enjoy it!

1   The development of 14–19 education

What is Chapter 1 about?

This chapter will provide an overview of the historical development of 14–19 education and the key issues that have affected the current climate. We will also briefly consider the possible impact of future changes in the sector. We consider what we mean by 14–19 education in its current form and we introduce the concepts of pedagogy and andragogy and their different roles in the sector. The chapter is enhanced by reflective tasks and further reading and will enable you to understand the development of the sector.

Task 1.1 Preliminary reading

Pring, R., Hayward, G., Hodgson, A. et al. (2009) *Education for All: The Future of Education and Training for 14–19-year-olds*. London: Routledge.

What is 14–19 education?

Traditionally, schools have taught up to the age of 16 in compulsory education, while colleges and sixth form colleges have taught from the age of 16 in post-compulsory education. However there has always been a crossover between the two. As we can see from the timeline on pages 8–10, 14 has always been a crucial time in the development of young people. This can be seen from the 1917 Lewis report which made it compulsory to stay on at school until the age of 14 to the 2009 Nuffield report which proposed fundamental changes to the education of 14–19-year-olds. Historically, for those young people unlikely to achieve 5 A*–C grades at GCSE, vocational provision has often been offered at the local college to prepare them for the world of work. These 14–16-year-olds who have attended colleges since the 1990s have often been seen as difficult to reach and in danger of dropping out of education all together. The schools have sent them to college in an attempt to keep them interested where they have traditionally followed courses in areas such as construction, catering and hair and beauty. Staff that have been given these groups to teach have received no special training and have often struggled to control behaviour and maintain achievement. These groups have been viewed as the 'worst' groups and have often been taught by the newest tutor. Unsurprisingly this has lead to disappointing results and a poor reputation for vocational options for 14-year-olds.

There are alternatives in our education system, such as Steiner Waldorf schools, which develop young people's vocational skills and focus on their emergent development as active citizens within their own communities. However such alternatives are few and normally fee paying and therefore only accessible to the minority.

Since 2002 the focus has been on giving all young people at the age of 14 a realistic choice of options which includes recently developed courses leading to specialist diplomas in some vocational areas. These specialist diplomas are delivered in partnership between schools, colleges and employers and are intended to provide consistent educational experiences for all 14–19-year-old learners. The idea is that young people move seamlessly between schools, colleges and workplaces and remain in education and training at least until the age of 18. However there are many factors that will influence the success of this concept, not least of which is the change of government to a Conservative/Liberal Democrat coalition.

Andragogy and pedagogy

As tutors/practitioners it is important to understand the differences between teaching a child (14–15), a young person (16–18) and an adult (19+) and to think about the tools and techniques we use. The different developmental stages that young people go through during this very difficult period in their lives need to be taken into consideration. Learners in each of these categories have specific needs and teaching them requires tutors to adapt their teaching techniques and to understand the different stages of development.

14–15-year-old learners often:

- find many faults with, and are embarrassed by, both parents;
- like to be busy and involved in many extracurricular activities;
- are very anxious to be liked;

- have a large and varied social circle which includes friends of both sexes;
- may be quarrelsome and reluctant to communicate;
- show a strong desire for independence; want to be free of family;
- find relationships with siblings may be better than with their parents;
- see friends as very important and may have one or two 'best friends';
- commonly opt for dating and romantic relationships;
- develop improved arguing skills (demonstrated often and with great passion);
- acquire improved reasoning skills;
- begin to learn to apply concepts to specific examples;
- learn to use deductive reasoning and make educated guesses;
- learn to reason through problems even in the absence of concrete events or examples;
- become able to construct hypothetical solutions to a problem and evaluate which is best;
- start to focus on future outcomes beginning with a present focus, mixed with some fantasy;
- learn to recognize that current actions can have an effect on the future;
- start to set personal goals (and may reject goals set by others);
- improve decision-making skills;
- begin independently to differentiate right from wrong and develop a conscience;
- learn to distinguish fact from opinion;
- learn to evaluate the credibility of various sources of information;
- become able to anticipate the consequences of different options;
- may challenge the assumptions and solutions presented by adults/tutors/practitioners.

16–18-year-old learners often:

- display many of the same behaviours as 14–16-year-old learners;
- challenge authority and oppose structure;
- need to know why they are being asked to do something;
- have an overwhelming desire for social acceptance from their peers;
- are trying to answer the question 'Who am I?', going through processes of identity testing and identity formation in an attempt to discover and clarify values while exploring all the possibilities of who they might become as adults. This can often be frustrating for

the adults who know them but as tutors/practitioners, we should be tolerant and accepting of the various identities they 'try on';

- move closer to being independent, autonomous beings, connected to but separate from others, in control of one's life but aware of limitations and boundaries.

19+ or adult learners often:

- learn best when they perceive the outcomes of the learning process as valuable, contributing to their own development, work success, and so on;
- have very different ideas about what is important to learn;
- are very different from each other. Adult learning groups are likely to be composed of persons of many different ages, backgrounds and education levels;
- have a broad, rich experience base to which to relate new learning;
- learn more slowly than young people, but learn just as well;
- are much more likely to reject or explain away new information that contradicts their beliefs;
- have well-formed expectations, which, unfortunately, are sometimes negative because they are based upon unpleasant past formal learning experiences;
- are more likely to have undergone a transformational learning process in order to return to education.

All learners are different and it is impossible to describe each stage definitively. We all know 14-year-olds who demonstrate all of the behaviour of adults, and adults who display the behaviour of 14-year-olds. But in general we can see that there is a staged development of independent learning and psychological development that takes place from the age of 14 through to adulthood. We need to be aware of these stages and factor them into our dealings with these learners.

An important theory for the teaching of young people and adults is the theory of andragogy, developed by Knowles and which he referred to as 'the art and science of teaching adults' as opposed to that of pedagogy, 'the art and science of teaching children'. It is important to note the difference between the two.

Knowles identified four ways in which adults were different from children in their learning:

1   Self concept: adult learners are self-directing, independent and responsible for their own learning.
2   Experience: adult learners have a reservoir of practical examples, skills and knowledge that can be drawn upon and reused in new learning situations.

3 A readiness to learn: adults are internally motivated to learn and participate actively in the learning process.
4 An orientation to learning: adults work best in environments where they can apply reasoning abilities.

(Knowles 1980: 43)

Although this theory can be criticized for a number of reasons, one of the key criticisms is that not all adults are self directed and motivated to learn. There is also not necessarily such a clear division between pedagogy and andragogy. Some adults prefer a pedagogical approach and many children prefer an andragogical approach. This area will be explored in more depth in Chapter 2.

Task 1.2

Think about your own experiences of teaching. Which age groups have you taught? Do you think there is a difference between teaching 14–15-year-olds as opposed to young people aged 16–18 or adults 19+?

The historical development of 14–19 education

The 14–19 phase has been described as a period of transition – from youth to adulthood, from compulsory schooling to employment for some, from compulsory schooling into post-compulsory education and training for others.

(Pring et al. 2005)

As will become clear from the timeline in Box 1.1, provision of education for 14–19-years-olds has been constantly changing and is still in a period of transition. Even as this book goes to press there is yet more change on the way, with a coalition government and further planned alterations to the existing curriculum.

While we may become used to constant change and adapting to different policies, the needs of our 14–19-year-old learners remain constant. Whatever changes are made to the curriculum, funding or providers of 14–19-year-old education, there will always be a need for staff in schools and colleges and training providers to deliver high quality education and training to meet the needs of these very complex learners.

Box 1.1   Timeline of key developments in 14–19 education

1917 Lewis Report proposed school leaving age of 14 with no exemptions, followed by attendance for at least 8 hours a week or 320 hours a year at day-continuation classes up to age 18.

1918 Education Act (The Fisher Act) implemented recommendations of 1917 Lewis Report. This wide-ranging act extended education provision. The school-leaving age was to be raised to 14 and all young workers were to be given right of access to day-release education (not immediately implemented). The leaving age was eventually raised by the 1921 Act.

1926 Hadow Report, *The Education of the Adolescent,* proposed junior and senior schools with transfer at age 11, secondary education for all, and increase in school leaving age to 15.

1956 Colleges of Advanced Technology were created as technical and FE colleges were upgraded to this status. In the mid-1960s most of these became 'new universities'.

1959 Crowther Report was a wide-ranging report on the education of 15–18-year-olds which recommended provision of FE for 15–18-year-olds, especially school-leavers. It questioned the value of day-release provision for apprenticeships.

1969 Haslegrave Report promoted technical and business education.

1973 the school leaving age was raised to 16.

1980 White Paper, *A New Training Initiative: A Programme for Action*, set out the first plans for the Youth Training Scheme (YTS).

1982 Technical and Vocational Education Initiative (TVEI) launched, which aimed to stimulate technical and vocational education for 14–18-year-olds, administered by Manpower Services Commission (MSC).

1983 TVEI pilot schemes began.

1985 Green Paper, *Education and Training for Young People*, announced major expansion of YTS from April 1986.

1988 Higginson Report carried out a review of A Levels.

1988 Youth Training Guarantee meant that all 16- and 17-year-olds were to be in education, employment or training.

1990 YTS was renamed Youth Training.

1992 Further and Higher Education Act removed FE and sixth form colleges from local authority control and established Further Education Funding Councils (FEFCs) and unified the funding of higher education under the Higher Education Funding Councils (HEFCs), as well as introducing competition for funding between institutions and abolishing the Council for National Academic Awards.

1993 National Commission on Education (independent of government) published its final report *Learning to Succeed: A Radical Look at Education Today and a Strategy for the Future*.

1994 Modern Apprenticeships pilot schemes were announced.

1995 Modern Apprenticeships introduced.

1995 Youth Credits were introduced and the Youth Training name was dropped.

1996 Tomlinson Report dealt with inclusive education in FE.

1996 Dearing Report reviewed vocational qualifications for 16–19-year-olds but its recommendations were largely ignored.

1996 Jobseekers Act laid down rules about the relationship between study and eligibility for the Job Seeker's Allowance.

1997 Education Act was wide ranging but much watered down because of the forthcoming general election. It abolished the National Council for Vocational Qualifications (NCVQ) and the School Curriculum and Assessment Authority (SCAA) and replaced them with the Qualifications and Curriculum Authority (QCA).

1997 Investing in Young People announced by DfEE with its aim to increase participation in post-16 education.

1999 Modern Apprenticeships were expanded to 82,000 places. Investors in Young People was developed further and renamed ConneXions.

1999 Moser Report, *Improving Literacy and Numeracy: A Fresh Start*, concerned itself with National Literacy Strategy and National Learning Targets.

1999 Education Maintenance Allowance (EMA) pilot schemes aimed at greater take-up of and achievement in post-16 education.

2002 The 14–19 Green Paper, *Education: Extending Opportunities, Raising Standards*, proposed a new 14–19 phase offering more vocational choice at 14 with specialist diplomas.

2003 Green Paper, *Every Child Matters*, led to the 2004 Children Act.

2004 Tomlinson Report, *14–19 Curriculum and Qualifications Reform*, was a report of the working group chaired by former chief inspector Mike Tomlinson.

(*continued*)

2005 White Paper, *14–19 Education and Skills*, rejected some of 2004 Tomlinson Report's recommendations and introduced the concept of the specialist diplomas.

2006 Leitch Report, on prosperity for all in the global economy, highlighted the notion of world class skills.

2006 Framework for Excellence was about benchmarking the quality of provision.

2007 Teaching 2020 was a paper setting out the government's vision for schooling in the future.

2007 School leaving age was announced as rising to 18, to be implemented from 2013.

2008 14–19 Specialist diplomas were introduced to bring more vocational options to young people.

2008 Machinery of Governance proposed changes to funding and abolition of the Learning and Skills Council (LSC).

2009 The Nuffield Report, *Education for All, The Future of Education and Training for 14–19-year-olds* provided an overview of 14–19 education and made suggestions for the coming decade.

2009 Skills for Growth White Paper on investing in skills and the introduction of skills accounts.

2010 Qualifications Curriculum Framework (QCF) set out to deliver flexibility in the curriculum. It introduced the personal learning record.

2010 New coalition government intending to make changes to 14–19 diplomas.

As we can see there have been many reports and legislative changes designed to engage 14–19-year-olds and to increase participation in education and training among this age group. Throughout this timeline it is clear how pivotal '14' appears to be as a decisive age for life-changing decisions and educational practices.

We have chosen to focus on four of the most recent initiatives in order to give some indication of the current climate. We are aware that these things can change quickly but the messages and aims behind them remain. We are going to look more closely at both of the Tomlinson reports, the Leitch report and the Nuffield review.

The Tomlinson Report, 1996

Inclusion in further education (FE) is based on the concept of inclusive learning and not on the traditional discourse of inclusion/integration usually used in schools education. This often involves notions of social acceptance and belonging. Inclusive learning in FE was introduced by John Tomlinson in the Tomlinson report 1996, published by the FEFC Learning Difficulties and Disability Committee. The concept is defined as follows:

> Inclusive learning is a way of thinking about further education that uses a revitalized understanding of learning and the learner's requirements as its starting point. The aim is not for students simply to 'take part' in further education but to be actively included and fully engaged in their learning. By 'inclusive learning' therefore, we mean the greatest degree of match or fit between the individual learner's requirements and the provision that is made for them.
>
> (FEFC 1996a: 32)

The report's proposals were aimed at improving FE's response to learners with physical or learning disabilities, and at matching provision to a wider range of individual learning needs. It challenges the deficit model of the learner, and stresses the responsibility of the college or other educational institution to take into account the requirements of each individual.

The report also introduces the term 'inclusive learning' to describe the move to provide education for all learners that is suitable and fit for purpose. Inclusive learning is a term designed to address the need to ensure that people can have access to further education and training, despite any learning or physical disability that they may have. The Tomlinson report has been influential in promoting a learner-centred approach to further education and training which goes beyond the original remit of addressing the needs of people with learning difficulties and physical disabilities.

A key part of the report was that students with any learning or physical disability should not be seen as having problems, i.e. a deficit model. Rather it promoted the need to focus on what institutions can do to respond to individual student requirements. This approach was intended to ensure that people were not labelled and would be enabled to learn to the best of their abilities (see Hillier 2005). 'Put simply, we want to avoid a viewpoint which locates the difficulty of deficit with the student and focuses instead on the capacity of the educational institution to understand and respond to the individual learner's requirements and see people with disabilities and/or learning difficulties first and foremost as learners' (FEFC 1996a: 2). No longer would students be expected to adapt to the requirements of the currently constructed Post Compulsory Education and Training (PCET) institutions. Rather PCET institutions would have to adapt to the needs of the learners coming through their doors. 'Participation must be widened, not simply increased' (Kennedy 1997). This means that the curriculum offer is of paramount importance to encourage learners to participate.

> It is arguably the curriculum which always stood – secure as a Berlin Wall – between mainstream and segregated special provision; it was the possibility of mediating that curriculum, and the means of its delivery, which enabled 'integrative' education; and it is still the curriculum on which the success of any truly inclusive initiative rests.
>
> (Clough and Corbett 2000: 21)

With the decline in the welfare state in which it was the responsibility of the government to provide all types of social welfare, including education, we have seen the 'state' abdicating some of its responsibilities for education. In the current climate the idea that the curriculum must meet social needs has become less important, and the idea of what 'needs' means has also changed. Need no longer refers to a generalized need of potential students, but to various 'special needs'. These include the needs of 14–16-year-old learners and those likely to disengage with education altogether.

So what does all this mean?

The Tomlinson report was vital in opening up the curriculum to meet the needs of each group of learners and not just those with traditional 'special needs'. The needs of 14–16-year-old students who were attempting to access the curriculum for vocational training were identified as being important and the curriculum and teaching techniques were adjusted to enable these young people to succeed on equal terms with the traditional post-16 learners. Colleges and schools were to work together to provide meaningful options for these young people rather than expecting them to fit in with the existing curriculum.

It also meant that education providers needed to consider the curriculum offered for all. Rather than offer the same old options they needed to identify what learners and employers actually wanted and provide courses in those areas.

Further education colleges have come a long way since the Tomlinson report in their efforts to provide inclusive learning for all groups and communities. The FE classroom includes a much wider range of students who are all catered for and their individual needs assessed and addressed. Support for learning has been fundamental in addressing these changes, as has the changing ethos and environment in FE colleges. However, despite the policy push for inclusion and lifelong learning, there is still evidence of a learning divide.

Tomlinson (1996), Kennedy (1997) and Moser (1999) made a strong call for widening participation in FE for groups who have traditionally been excluded. However, with the pressure on FE colleges to engage in a market economy and to organize courses for profit it is difficult to see how they can maintain this commitment to the community and its diverse needs.

Colleges are in an arena in which there is a constant tension between social inclusion/inclusive learning and economic pressures. The resulting conflicting forces are still being negotiated by both staff and communities: 'The resource demand of widening participation means that colleges are being responsive where resources are made available rather than starting from first principles with a review of what the most appropriate strategies may be within their own locality' (Lumby and Foskett 2005: 92).

In order to address the remaining conflicts we need to truly value education for all: 'Education has always been a source of social vitality and the more people we can include in the community of learning, the greater the benefits to us all. It is the likeliest means of creating a modern, well-skilled workforce, reducing levels of crime, and creating participating citizens' (Kennedy 1997: 16).

The Tomlinson Report, 2004

In 2004 Mike Tomlinson published his second major report into further education called *14–19 Curriculum and Qualifications Reform*.

The aim of this report was to address the problems of having too many qualifications that were not understood by either parents or employers. He suggested that the sector was over-burdened by examinations and a very complex curriculum offer. He suggested that there should be a new framework for qualifications where all qualifications were available in equal credit values and could be taken flexibly to make up an overall 'diploma,' 'certificate' or 'award'.

The aims of the report were to:

1 **raise participation and achievement** by tackling the educational causes of disengagement and underachievement and low post-16 participation;
2 **get the basics right** by ensuring that young people achieve specified levels in functional mathematics, literacy and communication and ICT, and are equipped with the knowledge, skills and attributes needed to succeed in adult life, further learning and employment;
3 **strengthen vocational routes** by improving the quality and status of vocational programmes delivered by schools, colleges

and training providers, setting out the features of high quality provision and identifying a clear role for employers;

4 **provide greater stretch and challenge** by ensuring opportunities for greater breadth and depth of learning. This will help employers and universities to differentiate more effectively between top performers. Stretch and challenge at all levels will encourage young people to think for themselves and be innovative and creative about their learning;

5 **reduce the assessment burden** for learners, tutors/practitioners, institutions and the system as a whole by reducing the number of times learners are examined; extending the role of tutor assessment; and changing assessment in A levels in order to improve the quality of teaching and learning;

6 **make the system more transparent and easier to understand** by rationalizing 14–19 curriculum and qualifications within a diploma framework, where progression routes and the value of qualifications are clear.

The proposals centred on linked developments. First, a common format for all 14–19 learning programmes which combines the knowledge and skills everybody needs for participation in a full adult life with disciplines chosen by the learner to meet their own interests, aptitudes and ambitions. Secondly, a unified framework of diplomas which provide a ready-made, easy-to-understand guarantee of the level and breadth of attainment achieved by each young person, whatever the nature of their programme. Finally, clear and transparent pathways through the 14–19 phase and progression into further and higher learning, training and employment, which are valued by employers and HE and motivate young people to stay on in learning after the age of 16.

So what does all this mean?

The findings of the review were discussed in the 2005 white paper *14–19 Education and Skills*, and it was decided to dilute some of Tomlinson's recommendations by retaining GCSEs and A levels as cornerstones of the new system. Tomlinson had advocated that GCSEs and A levels be phased out and academic diplomas introduced in their place.

However, much was retained from the report including the move to introduce new specialized vocational diplomas, including academic and vocational material, covering a key occupational sector of the economy. The diplomas would be available at levels 1 (foundation), 2 (GCSE) and 3 (advanced). They would introduce the diplomas in 14 areas and make these a national entitlement by 2015. The first four diplomas in information and communication technology, engineering, health and social care, and creative and media were to be ready in 2008. Eight more were selected to be available by 2010.

These diplomas are currently in process of being introduced and as yet there is little data available on the success of this initiative. What we do know is that they have been fundamental in highlighting the 14–19 debate and in encouraging collaboration and meaningful working between schools and colleges for the benefit of young people. Whatever the future holds for the specialized diplomas it is certain that the provision of vocational options and transitions at the age of 14 will continue to occupy the minds of future governments and policy-makers.

The Leitch Report, 2006

This review recommended that the UK commits to becoming a world leader in skills by 2020, benchmarked against the upper quartile of the Organisation for Economic Co-operation and Development (OECD). This means doubling attainment at most levels. The objectives outlined for 2020 include the following:

1   95 per cent of adults should achieve the basic skills of functional literacy and numeracy, an increase from levels of 85 per cent literacy and 79 per cent numeracy in 2005.
2   Over 90 per cent of adults should be qualified to at least Level 2, an increase from 69 per cent in 2005. There is a commitment to go further and achieve 95 per cent as soon as possible.
3   There should be a shift in the balance of intermediate skills from Level 2 to Level 3. This should improve the esteem, quantity and quality of intermediate skills. The result should be 1.9 million additional Level 3 attainments over the period and an increase in the number of apprentices to 500,000 a year.
4   Another target is to have 40 per cent of adults qualified to Level 4 and above, up from 29 per cent in 2005, with a commitment to continue progression.

As well as these ambitious objectives, the following principles were intended to underpin the delivery of this ambition:

Shared responsibility: employers, individuals and the government must increase action and investment. Employers and individuals should contribute most where they derive the greatest private returns. Government investment must focus on market failures, ensuring a basic platform of skills for all, targeting help where it is needed most.

Focus on economically valuable skills: skill developments must provide real returns for individuals, employers and society. Wherever possible, skills should be portable to deliver mobility in the labour market for individuals and employers.

Demand-led skills: the skills system must meet the needs of individuals and employers. Vocational skills must be demand led rather than centrally planned.

Adapt and respond: no one can accurately predict future demand for particular skill types. The framework must adapt and respond to future market needs, and build on existing structures. We should avoid the temptation to chop and change. Instead, performance of current structures should be improved through simplification and rationalization, stronger performance management and clearer remits. Continuity is important.

Main recommendations

In addition to the principles outlined above the report made some specific and wide-ranging recommendations:

1   Increase adult skills across all levels. Progress towards world class is best measured by the number of people increasing skills attainment. The raised ambitions will require additional investment by the state, employers and individuals. The government is committed to increasing the share of GDP for education and skills.
2   Route all public funding for adult vocational skills in England, apart from community learning, through Train to Gain and Learner Accounts by 2010.
3   Strengthen the employer voice. Rationalize existing bodies, strengthen the collective voice and better articulate employer views on skills by creating a new Commission for Employment and Skills, reporting to central government and the devolved administrations. The Commission will manage employer influence on skills, within a national framework of individual rights and responsibilities.
4   Increase employer engagement and investment in skills. Reform, re-license and empower Sector Skills Councils (SSCs). Deliver more economically valuable skills by allowing public funding for vocational qualifications only where the content has been approved by SSCs.

5   Launch a 'pledge' for employers voluntarily to train all eligible employees up to Level 2 in the workplace. In 2010, review progress of employer delivery. If the improvement rate is insufficient, introduce a statutory entitlement to workplace training at Level 2 in consultation with employers and unions.

6   Increase employer investment in Level 3 and 4 qualifications in the workplace. Extend Train to Gain to higher levels. Dramatically increase apprenticeship volumes. Improve engagement between employers and universities. Increase co-founded workplace degrees. Increase focus on skills at Level 5 and above.

7   Increase people's aspirations and awareness of the value of skills to them and their families. Create high-profile, sustained awareness programmes. Rationalize existing fragmented 'information silos' and develop a new universal adult careers service.

8   Create a new integrated employment and skills service, based upon existing structures, to increase sustainable employment and progression. Launch a programme to improve basic skills for those out of work, embedding this support for disadvantaged people and repeat claimants. Develop a network of employer-led Employment and Skills Boards, building on current models, to influence delivery.

So what does all this mean?

Lord Leitch suggests that we need to focus on the development of vocational skills and work-related curricula in order to meet the country's emerging skills gap. The workplace is constantly changing and the jobs that our children and grandchildren will do may not yet exist or even be required in the current climate. So how do we as educators design a curriculum that trains people to do these non-existent jobs?

Many authors (including Giddens 1998 and Leadbeater 2000, cited in Pring et al. 2009) have espoused the view that there is a need to train our young people to do high-level jobs that are not yet thought of and contend that globalization and technological change are inevitably driving the economy in this direction. However, what they seem to ignore is that there is an ever-widening pool of low-paid jobs at the bottom of the labour market for which it is difficult to find workers. Do we raise expectations unnecessarily by over-training our young people for them to be condemned to low-paid and often part-time employment?

Additionally, the number of graduate vacancies has fallen by nearly 7 per cent in 2010 according to the Association of Graduate Recruiters (AGR). This reported decrease follows a drop of 8.9 per cent in 2009. The median graduate starting salary has also failed to rise and remains at the

2008 figure of £25,000. Even though the number of job vacancies is falling the number of people going to university has been radically increasing. There were 334,594 accepted applicants according to UCAS in 1999, yet ten years later in 2009 there were 481,854 – an increase of 44 per cent and an increase of 25,227 (5.5 per cent) on entry for 2008. There was an overall increase in the number of applicants of 8.7 per cent. Applicants aged 20 and under showed a 6.9 per cent increase.

Mary Curnock Cook, UCAS Chief Executive, commented (Curnock Cook 2010):

> 2009 saw an unprecedented demand for places at university or college, but significantly more students have been accepted into higher education than ever before. Whilst there have been increases across the board, our figures show that there has been a particularly large increase in applicants aged 25 years and over – 89,133 in 2009, compared to 77,286 in 2008 – a 15.3 per cent increase. Males aged 25 and over have seen the biggest rise in acceptances – up 10.8 per cent to 20,963.

According to Leitch, by focusing on the development of vocational education that meets the needs of employers 'in terms of skills, deficiencies will reduce. Upskilling and portable, economically valuable qualifications throughout the entire workforce will ensure improved labour supply'.

It is true that this report has had a significant impact on 14–19 education in as much as the spotlight has been well and truly focused on skills and workplace training. Young people are being given the opportunity to undertake qualifications that are based in the workplace from the age of 14. However there is still the challenge of overcoming the belief that these opportunities are only of benefit to those low achievers who might not achieve five or more grade A–C GCSEs.

The Nuffield Review

There are two key questions at the heart of the ongoing debate about education and training for all young people, irrespective of background, ability or attainment:

- What counts as an educated 19-year-old today?
- Are the models of education we have inherited from the past sufficient to meet the needs of all young people, as well as the social and economic needs of the wider community?

These questions were addressed in the light of evidence collected over five years by the Nuffield Review of 14–19 Education and Training: the most rigorous investigation of every aspect of this key educational phase for decades. This review gives an overview of 14–19 education and training and makes suggestions for the kind of education and training that should be provided over the coming decade and beyond.

The review, in looking to the future and in the light of accumulated evidence, makes five over-arching demands:

1 *The re-assertion of a broader vision of education* in which there is a profound respect for the whole person (not just the narrowly conceived 'intellectual excellence' or 'skills for economic prosperity'). This must operate irrespective of ability or cultural and social background, and be based on a broader vision of learning, learning which contributes to a more just and cohesive society.

2 *System performance indicators 'fit for purpose'* in which the 'measures of success' reflect this range of educational aims, not simply those which are easy to measure or which please certain stakeholders only.

3 *The re-distribution of power and decision-making* such that there can be greater room for the voice of the learner, for the expertise of the tutor and for the concerns of other stakeholders with regard to the learning needs of all young people in their different economic and social settings.

4 *The creation of strongly collaborative local learning systems* in which schools, colleges, higher education institutions, the youth service, independent training providers, employers and voluntary bodies can work together for the common good. This collaboration will extend to curriculum development, provision of opportunities for all learners in a locality, and ensuring appropriate progression into further education, training and employment.

5 *The development of a more unified system of qualifications* which meets the diverse talents of young people, the different levels and styles of learning, and the varied needs of the wider community, but which avoids the fragmentation, divisiveness and inequalities to which the present system is prone.

So what does all this mean?

The Nuffield Review aims to understand the specific needs of 14–19-year-old learners in a changing society and global economy. There is an increasing number of young people not in education, employment or training

(NEETs) and the review seeks to find a solution for this phenomenon. The report concludes that more vocational education is the solution for some of these learners. More inclusive education is also advocated to extend opportunities and hope for our young people. The review concludes that a lot rests on the quality as well as the breadth of the provision offered.

We need to be able to include all learners, challenge the more able and support those with specific learning needs to achieve to their maximum potential. However, as always, there are areas of concern, not least of which is the need for organizations to work collaboratively for the good of young people even when there is no parity of esteem, pay, or conditions of service.

It is important also to note that many of the solutions offered by the review are not new but have been tried before. We need therefore to learn the lessons of the past in order to be able to meet the needs of the future.

Many of these solutions have failed in the past due to lack of funding or because rapidly-changing initiatives have rushed from one suggested solution to another. Any planned change to education needs to be given the time and the resources to succeed before we rush headlong into the next solution, as this has been the biggest stumbling block to effective reform over the last 30 years.

Task 1.3

How do you think these initiatives have changed the experiences of your learners?

1 Are you experiencing more 14–16-year-olds in your organization?
2 How does this impact on your teaching?

Task 1.4

1 Make a list of all the things that your learners want from you, the tutor.
2 Are you meeting all of these needs?
3 Is it possible to meet all of these needs?
4 What else can you do to give your learners a better experience?
5 How do you expect things to change in the future?

Possible future developments

The new government has announced its plans including the following statement taken from their website (August 2010):

We propose a revolution in skills and training, with:

- **A massive expansion in the provision of real apprenticeships**
- Measures to make it easier for companies to run apprenticeships
- Creating 100,000 additional apprenticeships every year with a £775 million injection of funds
- A £2,000 bonus for each apprenticeship at a small or medium-sized enterprise
- **More community learning to improve skills and employability**
- A £100 million NEETs fund aimed at youngsters not in any kind of education, training or employment
- A £100 million injection into the adult community learning fund
- **Supply-side reform to set further education fund**
- Freeing Further Education colleges from unnecessary bureaucracy
- Allowing new providers to enter the sector
- **A revolution in careers advice**
- Providing a careers adviser in every secondary school and college in the country
- Creating a new all-age careers advice service

Although some of these plans echo aspects of the Tomlinson, Leitch and Nuffield reviews it is possible that another rapid change of direction is on its way, as the new government seeks to make education its own and undo some of the changes made by the previous administration.

It is already expected that there will be changes to the specialist diplomas and the provision offered to 14-year-olds. Yet it is clearly evident that there will be provision of education for 14–19-year-olds and it will be delivered in partnership between schools, colleges and employers.

Chapter summary

This chapter has focused on the learners and their specific needs and desires rather than particular programmes or curricula. Whatever the curriculum, the needs and interests of these learners will remain the same and our ability to understand them, empathize with their issues and concerns and enhance their learning, will be paramount in our teaching. By understanding the specific stages of development we can use emotional intelligence to engage with our young people on an individual basis and to help them to maximize their potential and achieve their goals.

The chapter has also focused on the historical development of 14–19 education and has been informed by three key governmental reports that necessitated a thorough understanding of teaching and learning within this age range. The reports themselves have been instrumental in understanding why there has been disengagement and underachievement among young learners and have suggested a more meaningful approach to their education and training.

Further reading

Hodgson, A. and Spours, K. (2008) *Education & Training 14–19: Curriculum, Qualifications and Organisation*. London: Sage.

Lumby, J. and Foskett, N. (2005) *14–19 Education Policy, Leadership and Learning*. London: Sage.

2 Approaches to learning

What is Chapter 2 about?

In this chapter you can engage with the learning theories that underpin the 14–19 educational transition and develop models of practice relevant to your own educational setting, through tasks and exercises suitable for self and group study. Andragogy (adult learning) and pedagogy (child learning) are clearly explained as the two predominant, overarching approaches to learning and teaching and there are opportunities to examine the relevant and most useful aspects of both. You will also read about and examine other models of learning including the notion of personalized learning. Tasks and research suggestions assist you in effectively engaging with these concepts. Such suggestions will encourage interaction and consultation with your learners and their experiences which in turn will support your practical and 'applied' learning.

Task 2.1 Preliminary reading

Knowles, M. (1980) *The Modern Practice of Adult Education: From Pedagogy to Andragogy*. Chicago, IL: Fouett.

Introduction

One of the challenges of learning and teaching in the 14–19 age range, in other words post-compulsory education and training (PCET), has effectively been the acknowledgement of the 14–19 educational transition and especially 14–16-year-olds not only in terms of appropriate pedagogy but also in terms of collaborative management of that delivery.

Personalized learning has also had an increasingly important role to play, drawing on the following ethos. It is not always about fitting curriculum, teaching and assessment to the individual as many groups share very common characteristics; it is about developing social practices that enable people to become all that they are capable of becoming and that can be achieved in shared, collaborative team work and expression.

Transition from one learning environment to another has always been a particularly problematic feature of PCET in terms of its impact on the learner moving from school into a college environment. This chapter will, therefore, explore how this transition is possibly more acutely felt now that PCET has begun to embrace the notion of 14–19 education. It will argue that the 14–16-year-old, particularly, has had an education which has been influenced by a pedagogical learning and teaching approach and during transition to PCET they are then introduced to an andragogical methodology (Knowles 1984). So key questions to ask ourselves will be: What makes the 14–16-year-old distinctive as a potential learner in PCET? What are the differences between andragogy and pedagogy? How can knowledge and understanding of pedagogy and andragogy influence our approaches to planning for learning and therefore help us appreciate how 14–16-year-olds learn best? In all we will look at how to provide an effective and productive learning environment for all learners and discuss the role of the tutor in this delivery.

Task 2.2

1 Identify a group or cohort of 14–16-year-olds and write a short data profile giving details of what you know about the individuals and their attitude towards learning.
2 Identify some general headings for the information you have obtained, for example autonomous/dependent, prepared/unprepared, active learners/passive learners, etc.
3 Now identify a group or cohort of 16–19-year-olds with which you are familiar and compose a similar data profile. Are there similarities and/or differences?

It is likely that you will have observed and written down many differences and similarities and it will be these that will inform the next section of this chapter so note them down to return to later.

Reflecting on pedagogy and andragogy in the classroom

Task 2.3

1 Here are some descriptions of how a pedagogical approach to learning and teaching is perceived:
   - classroom environment: tense, low trust, formal, cold, aloof, authority-oriented, competitive, judgemental
   - learners: dependent personality, subject-centred, motivated by external rewards and punishment
   - objective setting, planning and assessment primarily carried out by the tutor.

2 Here are some descriptions of how an andragogical approach to learning and teaching is perceived:
   - classroom environment: relaxed, trusting, mutually respectful, informal, warm, collaborative, supportive
   - learners: increasingly self-directing, a rich resource for learning by self and others, task- or problem-centred, motivated by internal incentives, curiosity
   - objective setting, planning and assessment carried out mutually by learners and facilitator and by mutual negotiation with learner-collected evidence validated by peers, facilitators, experts.

Reflecting on your own learning and teaching experiences, are there any of these descriptors of pedagogy and andragogy which you have observed and with which you agree? Why? Once you have completed and reflected on the tasks, would you agree that this is helpful in appreciating how 14–16-year-olds may feel as they make the transition from school to PCET?

Knowles (1984), one of the key proponents of the andragogical approach to learning and teaching, believed that our current practice of educational instruction which is heavily dependent on pedagogical principles creates 'dependent persons'. Have you noticed this in your 14–16 learners? He also believed that a practice of educational instruction moving towards andragogical principles would create 'mature persons'. Are 14–16-year-olds prepared for this?

Now let us consider Tasks 2.2 and 2.3 and the data from your observations and experiences in more detail to construct a clearer picture of your professional setting and how we might improve the transitions and

Table 2.1 Possible directions

From pedagogy	Towards andragogy
Dependence on others for educational ideas	Ability to identify and think about educational issues for oneself
Dependence on tutor/practitioner	Autonomous learner
Passive conformity to learning	Creative quest for continuously more effective ways to translate educational ideas into learning
Narrow interest in learning	Constantly expanding interest in learning
Tutor/practitioner plans content	Learning contracts, projects
Logical sequence	Sequenced by readiness
Tutor/practitioner orientated objectives	Mutually negotiated objectives
Tutor/practitioner directed assessment	Learner – collected evidence validated by peers, facilitators and experts

the learning experiences of 14–16-year-olds. Table 2.1 indicates possible directions we might consider. Study this carefully and then undertake Tasks 2.4 and 2.5.

Task 2.4

1 In what ways have you noticed how dependency on the part of your learners manifests itself? Compare and contrast this with the two groups/ cohorts you identified earlier.
2 Are the learners generally passive in class? If so how does this affect your role?

Perhaps you are now appreciating that the two models of teaching discussed are in fact two rather extreme examples of each model. Pedagogy embodies an instructor-focused education where tutors assume responsibility about what will be learned, how and also when it will be learned. Dewey (1938) was one of several educators who believed that it fell short of its potential and stressed the importance of learning by doing, of learning from guidance, thus promoting a learner-centred educational philosophy.

Before we move on to look at the implications for planning (in Chapter 3), it would be useful to stress that we are looking at a transitional element in the move towards andragogy; in other words a mixture of the two approaches which seeks to serve the interests of both tutors and learners and promote successful learning and teaching.

Task 2.5

Consider the statements made in Case Study 2.1 and suggest reasons from a learning and teaching perspective why this particular choice to study in Year 10 at a local college was right for Elisabeth.

Case Study 2.1 Elisabeth

14–16 courses: Accounting
Now studying: International Baccalaureate Diploma
Previous school: Ambridge College of Arts

I chose the Accounting course to study in Year 10 because it was different from the traditional options at school. The course was really interesting, I learnt different things that I wouldn't have done in school and gained an insight into real job opportunities. I'm now studying the International Baccalaureate (IB) Diploma at my college, where I could achieve up to 6 A Levels at grade A. It's a challenging course but I feel that studying the Accounting course first prepared me for it; I developed better time management skills which were really useful when I started on the IB Diploma.

Meet Elisabeth's mum

College has been really good for Elisabeth. She met lots of different people from all sorts of diverse backgrounds. The skills that she learnt on the Accounting course have helped her with her studies now. The tutors were very supportive and gave regular feedback on Elisabeth's progress. I think that any parent who is a bit nervous about allowing their child to attend college shouldn't worry. Your child will get more opportunities to study the things they're really interested in.

If we summarize the main positive features we arrive at a clear model for success when planning for learning in the 14–16 age range. From the learner's perspective the following are important:

- choice
- different
- interesting

- non-traditional
- challenging
- useful skills.

From the tutor's perspective the following are the positives:

- supportive
- regular feedback
- diversity of learners and backgrounds
- study skills
- interesting.

Models of learning

It would be inappropriate to suggest that learning in a school environment is the antithesis of the above perspectives, but it is nonetheless very pertinent that learners in the 14–16 age range should view the PCET environment as useful, challenging, interesting and so on. In our view learning and teaching in schools and colleges are dominated to varying degrees by the three models of learning outlined below, with a more detailed discussion later on in this chapter.

1 Behaviourist model

Key figures: Pavlov, Thorndike and B.F. Skinner
Basic assumption: the human is a machine and learning is programming the machine.
Role of the tutor: the authority figure (programmer, tutor and instructor) determines and describes acceptable and appropriate behaviours.
Teaching strategies: mechanistic strategies are used to programme the learner and elicit behaviour (behaviour modification).

2 Cognitive model

Key figures: Jerome Bruner and David Ausuebel
Basic assumption: the human is a brain and learning is developing brain skills such as critical thinking and problem solving.
Role of the tutor: the tutor works to develop the brain to think critically.
Teaching strategies: thinking strategies are paramount in instructional practice.

3 Humanist model

Key figures: Abraham Maslow and Carl Rogers (and the humanists)
Basic assumption: the human is a unique creation.
Role of the tutor: the key purpose is to help each person to develop his or her unique potential.
Teaching strategies: the educational process includes self-directed learning or inquiry.

Why are there theories of learning?

In most life situations, learning is not much of a problem. Most people take it for granted that we learn from experience and see little that is problematic about learning. Throughout history people have learned, in most cases without troubling themselves as to the nature of the process. Parents have taught children and master workers have taught apprentices. Both learners and those who taught them felt little need for a grasp of learning theory. Teaching was done by 'teachers' telling and showing learners how, complimenting the learners when they did well and scolding or punishing them when they did poorly. Teachers simply taught the way that they had been taught as children or apprentices.

When schools were developed as special environments to facilitate learning, teaching ceased to be so simple. The subjects taught were different from the matters learned as part of routine life in a tribe or society. Mastering school subjects appeared to children as an entirely different sort of learning task from those taken for granted in everyday life. Often their relevance to the problems of daily living seemed unclear.

Ever since education became formalized in schools, teachers have been aware that learning in schools is frequently highly inefficient. For example, material to be learned may be presented to learners innumerable times without noticeable results. Many learners may appear uninterested; many may become rebellious and make serious trouble for teachers. Consequently, when teaching moved from the mother's knee to a formalized environment, it was inescapable that some people would begin speculating about whether schools were getting the best possible results. Then, professional psychologists and educators who critically analysed school practices found that development of more or less systematic schools of thought in psychology offered a handy tool for crystallization of their thinking. Each of these schools of thought has contained, explicitly or implicitly, a theory of learning. In turn, a given theory of learning has implied a set of classroom practices. Thus, the way in which educators build curriculas, select materials and choose instructional techniques depends, to a large degree, upon how they define 'learning'. Hence a theory of learning may function as an analytical tool, being used by its exponents to judge the quality of a particular situation.

There are no final answers to questions concerning learning and no theory can be found to be absolutely superior to all others. Nevertheless, tutors can develop learning theories of their own; such theories may turn out to be replicas of those we will look at.

Task 2.6

How did you learn to do the following?

- drive a car
- memorize lines in a play or song
- wire an electric plug
- dance
- not to let a match burn right down
- wear old clothes when decorating
- speak a foreign language
- operate a digital recorder
- become a specialist in your subject

What do we mean by learning?

Sometimes the word is used simply as an alternative to 'memorize' or 'learn by heart' – 'take this home and learn it'. More usually it carries an implication of change, either in knowledge or behaviour. But change is not necessarily the result of learning – age produces change in us. Learning as a form of change may be more or less automatic responses to new information, perception or activities (for example, learning that a hot plate burns). This we call incidental learning. Or it may be the result of structured, purposeful changes which extend our ability to do something. For this change to happen there needs to be a process of reception and engagement with the new material and a process of responding to it. We facilitate these processes by teaching.

Teaching styles

Most of us use a variety of styles, but which of the following do you think best describes what you do?

Tutor centred The tutor identifies the objectives, the pace and the content of learning and presents it to the learners in the form of a formally taught lesson or lecture. This is generally the easiest approach and may reflect the way we were taught. It is the easiest because it is tutor controlled. It can also reflect our feelings of status and power (the expert). At its best the charismatic tutor can communicate enthusiasm and knowledge; at its worst it becomes an ego-trip for the tutor and emphasizes the amount of teaching that goes into a session, rather than the amount of learning that comes out of it. All research suggests that on its own it is the least effective way of learning.

Learner centred The learners identify the objectives and the pace at which they are studying, through group discussion, negotiation with the tutor or their own choices in a flexible learning framework. Here the learner is in control, making his or her decisions about time, methods, and so on. It can be very demanding on the tutor as it requires a wider range of skills and the direction and content cannot be predicted. At its best it builds up learners' self esteem and knowledge application/skills. But it needs to be structured and facilitated carefully. At its worst it becomes chaotic and self-destructive – 'go away and do what you like'. Tutor laziness is not learner centredness.

Subject centred The subject is all. There isn't time in the course for anything other than the essential subject material. This needs assembling and structuring – delivery may be tutor centred or resource centred. This puts the emphasis on the nature of the subject and the mental processes required to internalize the new knowledge and use it – is knowledge any use unless it is applied? The emphasis is upon careful structuring of the learning process and the development of higher level skills of analysis, concepts and application.

Activity centred The learners learn through practical activities which are repeated and developed. The practical activities may be set up and controlled by the tutor or initiated by the learner. We often learn by doing. Therefore, teaching may focus upon the development of skills through activity and experience. The strength of the learning is determined by the amount of reinforcement and practical experience. However, to work as a learning strategy it needs careful structuring so that lower-order skills are managed before higher ones are undertaken.

In very broad terms each of the above approaches can be seen in terms of particular groups of theories about how we learn:

Tutor centred – behaviourism
Learner centred – humanism

Subject centred – cognitive learning
Activity centred – experiential learning

We'll move on now to a more detailed discussion about each of these key approaches to learning.

Behaviourism

We learn by receiving a stimulus from our environment and this stimulus produces a response (remember Pavlov and his dogs!). The tutor selects the stimulus and reinforces approved responses by rewarding students and discouraging the wrong responses by disapproval. For example, at its crudest level this could be by doling out sweets and detentions or at a more subtle level by a more complicated system of success indicators and body language. Feedback, the return from learner to tutor, is largely related to the reward. Behaviourism is fundamental to most of our teaching – we usually define objectives in behavioural terms (e.g. learners should be able to ...). It underpins other approaches too as they all involve a stimulus–response model to some degree.

The approach's key features are that learning is strengthened by pleasure, reward and satisfaction. Learning is a change in behaviour. Tutor behaviour and non-verbal communication, conditioning and the class environment are all important in this approach.

Cognitivism

Since the 1960s a number of theories have developed the ideas of behaviourism further by focusing on the activity of the learner in processing the response and on the nature of knowledge itself. Cognitivism stresses the way in which perceptions are organized in our heads to produce insight. Material must be marshalled in our heads step by step. Goals are set at each stage in the process and as we manage each stage we move to a higher level of activity. Feedback is an essential part of this process and not simply as a means of checking the response and giving approval or disapproval. So cognitivists see the learning steps as a series of upward movements or hierarchies. Some key models in this field are illustrated below:

Bloom's Cognitive Hierarchy
knowledge –> comprehension –> application –> analysis –> synthesis –> evaluation

Bloom's Affective Hierarchy
receiving –> responding –> valuing –> conceptualizing –> organizing

Gagne's Hierarchy

signal –> stimulus/response –> chaining –> verbal association –> multiple discrimination –> concept learning –> principle learning –> problem solving

Humanism

These theories are more recent in origin and stress the active nature of the learner, where the learner's actions largely create the learning situation. Such theories emphasize the importance of the urges and drives of the personality – for example, moving towards an increase in autonomy and competence; the active search for meaning; the goals that individuals set for themselves and the social setting within which they operate. Motivation for learning comes from within and the pace of learning is influenced by the whole of life, including the cultural and interpersonal relationships that form the social context. The role of the tutor is that of facilitator, enabling learners to increase their range of experience so that they can use it to achieve their desired learning changes. Humanism takes a holistic view of learning and is concerned with the person as a whole, with the idea of the learner's self-esteem seen as central.

Chapter summary

Pedagogy and andragogy are overarching approaches to learning and teaching and although they are open to interpretation and critique, we have attempted to present the approaches as clearly as possible, focusing utterly on their practical use to produce effective learning. Indeed andragogical approaches are already embedded in much of our work in PCET and the intention here is to help tutors appreciate that learners in transition from school will need careful introduction to the techniques associated with the approach.

Further reading

Fawbert, F. (2008) *Teaching in Post-compulsory Education: Skills, Standards and Lifelong Learning*. London: Continuum.

Knowles, M. (1994) *The Adult Learner: A Neglected Species*, 3rd edn. Houston, TX: Gulf Publishing Company.

3   Planning for learning

What is Chapter 3 about

This chapter considers planning for learning and in particular looks at what we mean by the terms 'learning objectives' or 'learning outcomes' and how we devise suitable objectives in our planning in the context of the three models discussed in Chapter 2. It is followed by a concise approach to formulating objectives within different learning domains, for example cognitive, behavioural and psychomotor. It then goes on to consider conditions for effective learning, personalized and differentiated learning, questioning and organizing the learning environment. The chapter aims to provide you with practical strategies to ensure effective learning, teaching and assessment in the classroom.

Task 3.1 Preliminary reading

Minton, D. (2005) *Teaching Skills in Further and Adult Education*. London: Thomson Learning.

What are objectives?

Whilst 'aims' are what you broadly intend to do as the tutor, 'objectives' are testable statements describing what you intend your learners to do. For example, the learner should be able to;

- use inverted commas correctly
- solder electronic components on to a circuit board
- state three advantages of the diesel engine over the petrol engine
- list the main methods of post management in Indonesia
- distinguish between fog, smog, mist and cloud.

These are much better than more tutor-centred aims such as 'to describe how to punctuate correctly' or 'to show learners how to solder'. If you think about these examples carefully, you will see that such aims can be satisfactorily met whether or not the learner has learned anything, so it is important to shift the focus from teaching to learning.

Shifting the focus from teaching to learning has a number of advantages. It makes clear what learners have to practise and helps us avoid a lesson dominated by tutor talk, where little real learning takes place. It makes lesson planning easier by suggesting suitable learning activities (for example corrected practice of soldering or dialogue writing). Moreover, if you know precisely what your learners should be able to do, it is much easier to assess whether or not they have achieved this, which in turn enables you to evaluate how successful your lessons have been.

Specific learning outcomes or specific objectives should:

- specify precisely and in concrete terms what the learner should be able to do;
- be written in such a way that it is possible to determine whether or not the objective has been achieved;
- usually be short term;
- be drawn up by the tutor to suit the resources, the tutor and the learners;
- optionally, define the circumstances under which the objective is to be demonstrated and/or what constitutes an achievement, for example 'translate passage 6d in less than five minutes, making fewer than four minor mistakes'.

Some tutors like the mnemonic SMART which stands for Specific, Measurable, Agreed, Realistic and Time bound.

Defining the two types of objectives

There are two main types of objectives – behavioural and non-behavioural. The key characteristics of behavioural objectives are that they specify the following:

- who is to perform the desired behaviour;
- the actual behaviour in clear and unambiguous terms;
- the conditions for the behaviour to be demonstrated;
- the standard used to determine success or failure.

Using behavioural objectives requires great care because it defines learning in one particular way (behaviourally) and requires tutors to be sure this is appropriate for the course and the intended learning.

Non-behavioural objectives may be more flexible and open-ended but still need expressing simply and linking to learning experiences. They allow for broader notions of learning to be used, not just behaviour.

Behavioural objectives might well be most effective when the subject matter and intended learning is skill based and can be demonstrated easily, or where overt writing or speaking can demonstrate appropriate levels of learning or where learners need small, behavioural stages brought into the subject matter to provide clear, attainable targets. Non-behavioural objectives might be best used when the intended learning is more complex or less specific, is developmental and almost impossible to view in terms of behaviour without reducing the learning to an absurd level.

Writing objectives

This section is particularly focused on formulating learning objectives within each of the learning domains identified by Bloom in his 'Taxonomy of Educational Objectives or Goals': the cognitive, the affective and the psychomotor.

The cognitive domain

Bloom arranged the categories which follow in order of difficulty with the easiest first. It is important to include the higher-order objectives in your teaching or these skills will not be developed. Despite criticism, these domains do provide a straightforward and practical structure of learning and can help in constructing objectives in each learning domain.

Knowledge
To be able to: state; recall; list; recognize; select; reproduce; draw...
For example: recall Newton's Laws of Motion.

Comprehension
To be able to: explain; describe reasons for; identify causes of; illustrate...
For example: to give reasons for seat belts by referring to Newton's Laws of Motion.

Application
To be able to: use; apply; construct; solve; select...
For example: to use Newton's Laws of Motion to solve simple problems.

Analysis
To be able to: break down; list component parts of; compare and contrast; differentiate between...
For example: to compare and contrast communism and democracy.

Synthesis (this involves choosing, using and putting together diverse skills, abilities and knowledge to accomplish a particular new task)
To be able to: summarize; generalize; argue; organize; design; explain the reason for...
For example: to explain the reasons for quality assurance and quality enhancement in PCET.

Evaluation
To be able to: judge; evaluate; give arguments for and against; criticize...
For example: to give arguments for and against capital punishment.

The affective domain

This domain concerns itself with attention, interest, awareness, aesthetic appreciation, moral, aesthetic and other attitudes, opinions, feelings or values. For example:

- listen to... to appreciate the importance of...
- to have an awareness of... to respond with personal feelings...
- to have an aesthetic appreciation of... to have a commitment towards...
- to recognize the moral dilemmas involved in...

The psychomotor domain

This includes motor skills or physical skills including sense perception, hand and eye co-ordination, and so on. For example: to plan; to draw; to throw; to weld...

Task 3.2

1 Note down instances or evidence of each model discussed in Chapter 2 (behaviourist, cognitive, humanist) in the learning and teaching which you carry out. It is likely that you will find evidence of learning objectives or outcomes primarily drawing on the behaviourist and cognitive models.
2 Can you provide any evidence of objectives which draw upon the humanist model in your learning and teaching?

Using appropriate language for objectives

To formulate a clear objective, verbs should be chosen which will allow the objectives to state clearly what the learner should be observed to do in order to achieve the objective. Therefore it is best to avoid verbs such as 'know', 'understand', 'comprehend', and 'appreciate'. Box 3.1 gives examples of verbs which can be used to formulate objectives or outcomes in the three domains we have discussed.

Box 3.1   Useful verbs for formulating objectives

1 Cognitive domain

Knowledge: the ability to remember information that has been learned.
Verbs: write; state; recall; recognize; select; reproduce; measure; define; describe; label; list; name.

Comprehension: the ability to take in the meaning of the information.
Verbs: identify; illustrate; represent; formulate; explain; contrast; infer; distinguish; give examples; convert; classify; indicate.

Application: the ability to use information that has been learned.
Verbs: predict; select; assess; find; show; use; solve; construct; compute; manipulate; operate; demonstrate.

Analysis: the ability to break up information and so understand its structure and organization.
Verbs: select; compare; separate; contrast; differentiate; break down; conclude; summarize; discriminate; appraise; justify; criticize.

Synthesis: the ability to link or put together information to form a whole out of the parts.
Verbs: summarize; argue; relate; précis; organize; revise; generalize; conclude; combine; modify; plan; compile; design.

Evaluation: the ability to judge the value of information for a specific purpose.
Verbs: judge; evaluate; support; attack; avoid; select; recognize; criticize; conclude; appraise; contrast; justify; decide; interpret; support.

2 Affective domain

Receiving: the ability to be aware that a thing exists.
Verbs: listen; accept; attend; perceive; be aware.

Responding: the ability to participate; to react as well as attend.
Verbs: state; select; answer; write; derive; develop; react.

Valuing: the ability to consider the value of some behaviour or object; the attitude to the subject in hand.
Verbs: accept; increase; participate; attain; decide; discuss; write'.

Organization: the ability to develop a consistent system of values.
Verbs: relate; associate; find; form; select.

Characterization: the ability to develop a system of values that allow the development of a characteristic, consistent and predictable way of life.
Verbs: change; demonstrate; develop; judge; identify; decide.

3 Psychomotor domain

Knowledge: the ability to know the simple, related steps of a skill.
Verbs: state; recall; recognize; describe; list; name.

Application: the ability to relate the elements of skill to more advanced problems.
Verbs: perform; use; manipulate; build; demonstrate; construct; operate.

Mastery: the ability to use the skill in new situations involving hitherto unknown variables.
Verbs: as above but with additions giving new conditions and standards.

Task 3.3

In your opinion do any of the domains sit comfortably within the overarching approaches of pedagogy and andragogy?

Given its focus on the development of the individual from dependent to non-dependent and self-directing learner, the humanist model and its approaches are at once seen to be equally concerned with self-actualization and the acquisition of knowledge. And you may therefore agree that the humanist approach does indeed sit comfortably with andragogy and its approaches.

Task 3.4

Now note down some suggestions for planning for learning in your own subject area drawing upon each domain in order to ensure productive sessions which meet the criteria described by Elisabeth in Chapter 2 (see page 27).

Effective learning

In this section we will consider conditions for effective learning, the principles of learning and teaching and then explore the roles of both the learner and the tutor.

Task 3.5 Quick quiz: how do I help my learners to learn in the classroom?

Do I use learning which involves:	Often	Sometimes	Never
Discussion groups			
Use of audio visual			
Lecture			
Learners teaching each other			
Demonstration			
Learners reading			
Learners practising by doing			

Conditions for effective learning

- Learners feel a need to learn.
- The learning environment is characterized by physical comfort, respect, mutual helpfulness, freedom of expression and acceptance of differences.

- Learners perceive the goals of a learning experience to be their goals.
- Learners accept a share of the responsibility for planning and operating a learning experience, and therefore have a feeling of commitment towards it.
- Learners participate actively in the learning process.
- The learning process is related to and makes use of the experience of the learner.
- Learners have a sense of progress towards their goals.

Principles of teaching and learning

1 The tutor exposes learners to new possibilities of self-fulfilment.
2 The tutor helps each learner to clarify his own aspirations for improved behaviour.
3 The tutor helps each learner diagnose the gap between his aspiration and his present level of performance.
4 The tutor helps the learners identify the life problems they have experienced because of gaps in their personal equipment.
5 The tutor provides physical conditions that are comfortable (as to seating, smoking, mutual trust, temperature, ventilation, lighting, decoration) and conducive to interaction (preferably no person sitting behind another person).
6 The tutor accepts each learner as a person of worth and respects their feelings and ideas.
7 The tutor seeks to build relationships of mutual trust and helpfulness among the learners by encouraging cooperative activities and refraining from judging.
8 The tutor exposes their own feelings and contributes their resources as a co-learner in the spirit of mutual enquiry.
9 The tutor involves the learners in a mutual process of formulating learning objectives in which the needs of the learners, of the institution, of the tutor, of the subject matter and of the society are taken into account.
10 The tutor shares their thinking about the options available in the designing of learning experiences and involves learners in their selection of materials and methods.
11 The tutor helps the learners to organize themselves (project groups, learning-teaching teams, independent study, etc.) to share responsibility in the process of mutual inquiry.
12 The tutor helps the learners exploit their own experiences as resources for learning through the use of such techniques as discussion, role playing, case method, and so on.

13   The tutor gears the presentation of his own resources to the levels of experience of his particular learners.

14   The tutor helps the learners to apply new learnings to their experience, and thus make the learnings more meaningful and integrated.

15   The tutor involves the learners in developing mutually acceptable criteria and methods of measuring progress towards the learning objectives.

16   The tutor helps the learners develop and apply procedures for self-evaluation according to these criteria.

You can see that the conditions and principles of learning are very much a feature of the andragogical approach.

Case study 3.1 Helen

Helen is a very experienced college lecturer and has been involved in the teaching of 14–16-year-olds in a college setting. She has made some very good suggestions for planning for learning using the cognitive approach and also provides us with an overview of the implications of using this model.

Planning a cognitive approach to learning and teaching

The three key ingredients of my lessons are the learning outcomes, plus activity, plus assessment (depending upon the learners and the content).

I find the following steps helpful when I am planning a lesson:

1   At the outset I always let the learners know what is expected of them and *why* what I have prepared in terms of learner-centred activity is important.

2   I find that this creates a meaningful learning context and enables my learners to engage more readily particularly if I refer to my Learning Outcomes from time to time.

3   I always recap previous learning and show how the new material is related.

4   Question and Answer (Q & A)* is a great technique for eliciting current knowledge.

5   I can therefore assess learners' responses and contributions.

As the session progresses and the learners begin to involve themselves in discussion and problem solving activity, I revisit the learning outcomes and introduce further 'cognitive' support to help them fulfil the tasks.

1   I remind the learners what the learning outcomes of the lesson are.
2   I now assess through Q & A the learners' ability to engage with the concepts and skills they will need in order to solve the problems/tasks.
3   I ask learners to recall the necessary concepts and skills.
4   I constantly facilitate the activities, intervening only to encourage the learners' thinking short of giving them the solution to the problem.
5   Finally, in order to meet the specific learning outcomes, I assess the learners' learning by requiring them to give a full demonstration of the solution to the given problem.

The following helps me to plan to ensure effective learning in the cognitive domain:

Time It is helpful to give an indication of the time that is likely to be needed for each learning objective to be met.

Content Key words are best to focus the learners on the knowledge to be learnt.

Tutor activity This should specify the learning and teaching strategies which are intended to be used during the lesson. If a question or questioning technique is to be used then key questions should be indicated.

Learner activity The roles played by learners should be clearly stated so that variety can be planned. Learners should have a change of activity at least every 10 minutes.

Resources All audio-visual materials should be checked for clarity and readability.

Implications of this model for learning and teaching

Helen has neatly summarized the implications of using this model and clearly stresses that a learner's ability to code information will depend on key characteristics of the lesson such as:

1   **Speed of delivery** There should be pauses to allow learners to 'think' and reflect.
2   **Appropriate facilitation of learning** There should be opportunity and time for learners to take note of key points.
3   **Voice modulations to emphasize main points** Provide clues as to what must be learnt.
4   **Explanation of new concepts in terms of familiar ones** New concepts must be firmly anchored to established ones.
5   **Emphasis on connection and difference between concepts and ideas discussed** New concepts are analysed in terms of similarities and differences with existing concepts.

6 **Provision of practical illustrations of new principles linked to the learners' own experiences** Strengthen links with earlier ideas and events – this maintains attention.
7 **Use of questions** The question and answer process strengthens inter-connections of knowledge; allows time for further reflection. It also maintains attention.
8 **Variety of sensory input, for example visual or digital audio resources** This maintains attention and allows time for further reflection or bringing notes up to date.

It is important that these key characteristics should form the basis of any lesson plan with sections for timing, pitch, pace and resources and so on.

Task 3.6

Consider Helen's suggestions and write down how you help learners learn in your sessions. Also consider which domain you wish to reach.

It is very likely that if your approach is to encourage learner activity then your role will be that of a guide or facilitator and this role is sometimes not easily adopted, especially if you are a tutor who does like to talk and enthuse about your subject. Yet we need to consider the learners and, as Helen suggests, how they need variety of activity with clear guidance and direction. We have already stated that most formal education in schools still focuses on the tutor (pedagogy) rather than the learner (andragogy) and depending on your subject and your context you may now be appreciating the value of adopting a mixture of both approaches. Learners within the 14–19 age range are likely to be more receptive to this mixture as it will incorporate for them the familiar with the unfamiliar and produce the positive reaction expressed by Elisabeth in Case study 2.1 in Chapter 2.

Personalized learning and differentiated learning

The notion of personalized learning draws on the idea that groups or cohorts of learners share very common characteristics and, if given the opportunity, such groups can work collaboratively to achieve their outcomes. However, when planning for learning, a variety of factors relating to each group and which can have either a positive or negative impact must be considered, for example prior experiences, resources, ethnicity, gender, special educational needs. At first this can be very daunting for even the most experienced practitioner but this can be alleviated when we consider that it is the teaching strategies which need to be flexible, adaptive or 'differentiated'. This involves intricate knowledge on the part of the tutor/practitioner of the group through a detailed cohort analysis and a clear overview of what you expect of the learners.

Case study 3.2 Joshua

Joshua is a tutor of Modern Languages/ESOL and Literacy in an FE college and has considerable experience of working across all age ranges and levels and often has young learners and adult learners in the same group. He has always tried to plan for effective learning by clearly differentiating the teaching strategies he uses:

Joshua says, I always use three little words when planning for differentiated learning and teaching activities – **must, should** and **could.** I look carefully at what I consider to be essential knowledge that I expect all learners **must** have. Then I consider any additional content that the majority **should** be able to handle with guidance and what my advanced learners **could** achieve if stretched and guided. I make sure that resources and materials are appropriate for the learners in terms of ease of access and readability and I allow extra time for some learners. If necessary I differentiate the learning outcomes; one example of this is when I ask each learner to produce a postcard with a message to a friend – some learners choose to write or word-process these using dictionaries. Others may work together using key words which I provide on small laminated squares which they piece together to form sentences for the message. Each square is coloured according to grammatical function, for example red for nouns, blue for verbs, green for adjectives and so on. So if the learning objective is 'All learners must produce a postcard with a message for a friend' then, in varying ways, this will be achieved.

Task 3.7

- Consider the strategies employed by Joshua and produce a differentiated plan for learning on a topic of your choice in your subject area. Clearly relate each outcome to the activities by indicating numerically the activity to the outcome for example LO 1 – learners work together to construct sentences. Which activities might require more attention and guidance from you during the lesson?

(continued)

- Consider a particular concept or aspect of the subject you teach and suggest differentiated approaches which help all your learners to understand it and to produce evidence of that understanding.

Learners require help and support in the way they approach their learning. The tutor's responsibility is to vary their teaching style to suit the needs of the learners and make the most of the subject and the available resources through differentiated activities. Equally the learner's responsibility is to seek opportunities to develop their capacity to learn by acquiring a range of appropriate study skills – in other words, to learn how to learn. Also known as metacognition, this involves learners taking control of their development and improving their ability to continue to learn. In turn, this helps move them towards autonomy and self-actualization in learning environments where they feel valued, encouraged and empowered.

Yet planning for learning in the 14–19 age range can sometimes be challenging for those practitioners who are faced with groups of learners who clearly do not want to be there or who have simply had no previous experience of effective and rewarding learning and teaching. The following case study is particularly pertinent and reveals how adopting a learner-centred, andragogical approach can yield success in terms of classroom activity and learner achievement.

Case study 3.3 Sandra

Sandra is a part-time tutor in an FE college in Merseyside. She has been given a group of 16–18-year-olds who are described as NEET (not in employment, education or training). The learners are described as under-achievers, that is to say, they have not attained grade Cs in their GCSEs and they have been previously excluded at school for bad behaviour. The main aim of the college programme is eventually to get the learners onto a mainstream place at college. The course is about life skills, in particular basic customer service, and is allocated 60 guided learning hours spread over 20 weeks:

Sandra says, the first thing that hit me was the behavioural issues ranging from bullying, not paying attention, swearing and threats but more so the complete lack of knowledge or awareness of personal and social skills. They were articulate enough particularly in what they didn't like or want and it was clear that they did not want to be in my class. I found it challenging trying to embellish my sessions with basic customer service skills especially as there seemed to be very little to put into such lengthy three hour sessions. Attention spans were often only a few minutes. However I decided quite early on that it would be best to speak to them about what they wanted or expected and how I could help them. Quite soon I noticed how they preferred to hear about my own considerable retail experience and engage in small group discussions involving question and answer. This improved their concentration in basic tasks. I also recognized that their cultural references were quite narrow and my introduction of e-learning tools such as websites, YouTube and interactive e-based activities such as quizzes and competitions made a notable improvement in their learning. Emulating the workplace and enacting scenarios proved to be particularly welcome as was their desire to ask questions and recognize the transferable skills they were gaining. I did not appreciate the NEET label and I was pleased with the name change to Step Up. A learner-centred, blended learning approach was beneficial and I was pleased when I discovered that many progressed onto college courses with real aspirations for the future. I feel, however, that the crucial part of my successfully enhancing learning was through allowing question and answer and much discussion.

Further discussion of how Sandra successfully employed question and answer as an effective learning method is to be found later on in Task 3.8 and she features again in Chapter 5 to show how she gained access to interactive online resources and other e-learning tools.

Questioning: andragogy and Socratic questioning

Andragogy moves from emphasizing 'someone teaching something to someone in a given context' to one that captures the essentials of the interaction in the following manner: 'someone learning something with someone and/or others in a given context that facilitates interaction'. Andragogy produces collaborative relationships among students and between the students and the tutor. What the class knows as a whole becomes more relevant. The emphasis shifts from the tutor's onto the learners' contributions to the group discussion and learning. This was clearly a feature of Helen's approach in Case study 3.1 and Sandra's approach in Case study 3.3, so it is crucial that we should review the type of questioning techniques open to us in the facilitation of effective learning. Socratic questioning is an effective tool so we will examine it briefly here.

Socratic questioning is a tutor-directed form of instruction in which questions are used as the sole method of teaching. The technique is used to help emphasize learning by placing learners in the position of having to recognize the limits of their knowledge or at least any perceived gaps in that knowledge. This should, in turn, motivate them to learn. However, this technique could easily backfire if not executed with care and sensitivity with both adult and young learners.

Knowles (1973) asserted that adults require certain environmental conditions in order to learn:

1   Adults need to be involved in the planning and evaluation of their instruction.
2   Experience (including mistakes) provides the basis for learning activities.
3   Adults are most interested in subjects that have immediate relevance to their job or personal life.
4   Adult learning is problem centred rather than content oriented.

Earlier we saw how these conditions, once implemented, helped Sandra in Case study 3.3 to manage her learning and teaching and how Helen in Case study 3.1 adopted these conditions (especially number 4 above) as a useful premise for learning. So what exactly is involved in this technique and what about the learners themselves?

The Socratic technique

Socrates was a classical Greek Athenian philosopher whose dialogues were recorded by Plato and in which questioning was used to determine current knowledge and also the extent of that knowledge. Although its modern day usage does not accurately reflect its historical one, it is nonetheless a useful tool in learning and teaching particularly through discussion. Knowles (1973) emphasized that adults are self directed and expect to take responsibility for decisions and therefore learning and teaching methodology must accommodate this fundamental aspect. In andragogical terms, teaching needs to focus more on the process and less on the content being taught. Strategies such as case studies, role-playing, simulations, discussions and self-evaluation are considered most useful. Although the content or subject matter should remain stimulating and interesting to the learners, the processes of learning become a pivotal feature in effective acquisition of knowledge. Tredway (1995) suggested that this method is in fact a planned and sequentially structured discourse geared towards actively involving and engaging learners as they relate the topic and activities to real life or indeed their own life experiences. So the basis of this method is twofold: (1) the tutor presents the topic accompanied by a set of pre-prepared questions, which is (2) designed to 'lead' the learners towards meeting the learning outcomes by drawing on their own experiences and current knowledge. This method could be referred to as 'inductive' or 'heuristic'[1] whereby the learners actively and collaboratively discover and acquire knowledge and more importantly, retain that knowledge.

Learner types

Since we are dealing with a technique proffered by Socrates it is perhaps useful to identify learner types in much the way he would have, using the original Greek words ascribed to typical learners who were participants in Socrates' discussions, namely:

- Meno: typically these learners do require an authority figure who will give them the answer as they passively sit often reacting negatively to questioning. They like to take notes and prefer lectures as a learning and teaching method.
- Plato: these learners are more willing to take control of their learning, preferring a tutor who sets the scene and lets them get on with it and a situation in which learning is negotiated. They engage in active learning and desire challenge.
- Gorgias: these learners prefer a facilitative approach from the tutor who is on hand to guide and advise and help the learner think and re-think the content or subject matter. They are comforted by the idea of contributing to class discussion without fear of ridicule. They need their confidence building and this approach is very helpful.
- Protagoras: these learners prefer a tutor who is both authoritative and highly supportive and who will deliver learning in an enthusiastic and motivating manner. They are the ones who may lack prior knowledge and experience and therefore quickly feel alienated by discussion if this is not carefully and sensitively handled.

It is crucial, therefore, that as tutors we quickly identify the types of learners we have in our classes particularly if we wish to adopt a Socratic questioning technique to enhance learning. Earlier we met Sandra who indeed quickly discovered and identified learner types in her class. Interestingly she identified them by allowing a question and answer session to take place and by then observing behaviour and responses. She also prepared an outline of how this questioning technique would help in planning for learning as in Case study 3.4.

Case study 3.4 Sandra

Sandra's planning for learning involves the following sequentially linked activities:

- I decide on the practices or concepts I want all my learners to eventually understand.
- I then think up a scenario typically related to retail in order to instigate a discussion.
- I produce a list of questions which I feel will help the learners understand the practices or concepts I want them to understand. My own considerable subject knowledge and experience also helps in planning for every eventuality. Therefore I have a bank of further questions and possible examples which will still keep a focus on the discussion.
- Next I am in the classroom and I introduce the scenario and literally ask 'what would you do in this situation?'
- I allow and respond appropriately to all answers and I never dismiss any, preferring instead that the learners discuss and debate them.
- Once I am satisfied that the discussion has resulted in a common understanding of the concepts and practices, I then add new and more intriguing elements to the scenario continuing to ask 'Now what would you do?' and as more elements are added 'What now?'
- At this point I would plan to enact the scenario in the way my learners have suggested if they are struggling. Questions like 'Is this the way you mean?', 'What would you further suggest or do in this situation?' are very useful. The discussion continues on track.
- Finally I summarize or recap all their suggestions or solutions to the scenario and stress that these are the learners' contributions and therefore the results of their knowledge and experiences. All this has been achieved by a carefully planned questioning technique.

Task 3.8

- Consider how Sandra has planned for learning with her group and draft a plan for your own which incorporates the use of the Socratic questioning technique. Remember to plan for every eventuality!

- Note down any observations you make which suggest that you are with learner types described earlier and how they respond to this technique.

The learning environment: room arrangement

The arrangement of a room can help or hinder the effectiveness of the management and process of learning. Consider all we have discussed in this chapter and you will certainly see that room layout is crucial to effective learning. Focus carefully on your own subject and look at the possibilities available. You may wish to look at the significance of room layout when using questioning techniques, group or pair work and discussion as effective learning and teaching methods.

Task 3.9

The following explore the suitability, or otherwise, of a variety of room arrangements. Using the space provided, indicate which arrangement(s) would be appropriate when you are teaching your subject.

1 Formal: learners sit in rows and face the tutor/practitioner who 'teaches' from the front

Advantages

- Traditional arrangements can suit certain types of subjects where it is not essential for learners to interact with each other.
- Learners can work better on individual projects or tasks.
- Some learners find the familiar setting a comfort – it is what they expect from a learning environment.
- Most teaching rooms lend themselves to this arrangement.

Disadvantages

- This arrangement may evoke unhappy memories of school.
- Some learners may not be able to see the tutor/practitioner or the visual aids.
- The tutor/practitioner cannot make eye contact with all the class, so some learners may feel left out.

(continued)

- Learners cannot make eye contact with other learners.
- Learners at the back of the class may engage in conversations not related to the lesson.

I would/would not use this layout because:

2 Oblong: the tables are set out in an oblong shape – the tutor/ practitioner delivers from the front but can move around the tables

Advantages

- The tutor/practitioner is part of the group.
- All members of the group are equally positioned.
- The tutor practitioner has easy access to all learners.

Disadvantages

- It is difficult to use visual aids, as some learners will have their backs to the board.
- Not all learners can see the tutor/practitioner.
- The arrangement needs a large room.

I would/would not use this layout because:

3 Half oblong: the tables are laid out as three sides of an oblong – the tutor/practitioner delivers from the empty side.

Advantages

- The tutor/practitioner can see all the learners.
- The learners can see the tutor/practitioner and the visual aids.
- The tutor/practitioner has easy access to learners and their work.
- The learners can see each other.

Disadvantages

- If the oblong is too big, the members at the far end may form their own group.
- Some learners may have to twist round in their seats to see visual aids.

I would/would not use this layout because:

4 Circle: the tables are set out in a circle – the tutor/practitioner delivers from the front but can move around the circle

Advantages

- The tutor/practitioner is part of the group; most of the group can see each other.
- An informal atmosphere is created.
- Eye contact can be made with most of the group.

Disadvantages

- Some learners might find it distracting, as they prefer to work alone.
- Not all learners can see the tutor/practitioner easily.
- It is difficult to use visual aids, as some learners would have to twist around in order to see them.

I would/would not use this layout because:

5 Semi-circle: the tables form a semi-circle around the tutor/ practitioner

Advantages

- The tutor/practitioner can see all the learners.
- All of the learners can see the tutor/practitioner and the visual aids.

Disadvantages

- Not all teaching rooms are big enough for this arrangement.
- Some learners cannot see each other.
- It is difficult to do with large groups.

I would/would not use this layout because:

6 Groups of tables: the tables are set out in small groups with space to talk between them

Advantages

- This is good for small group teaching.
- It fosters team spirit.
- It creates good table space for projects or practical work.
- It enables you to control who sits where.

Disadvantages

- It needs a large room to be successful.
- It can create a confusing environment.

(continued)

- It can make managing behaviour harder as you need eyes in the back of your head!

I would/would not use this layout because:

7 Semi-circle: seats only, no tables with seats laid out in a semi-circle

Advantages

- There are no barriers between tutor/practitioner and learners.
- It is good for discussion groups.
- It creates an informal environment.

Disadvantages

- It is a poor arrangement for note taking.
- It may be threatening to some learners, who need a table for protection.

I would/would not use this layout because:

It should now be clear that no one room arrangement can suit the requirements of all learners, subjects and learning outcomes. Reflect upon your last teaching session and complete Task 3.10

Task 3.10

Choose suitable room arrangements for your teaching, drawing on your conclusions from above. Complete the following:
In my subject area the following room arrangements would be appropriate:

	Yes	No
Formal		
Circle		
Semi-circle		
Half oblong		
Groups of tables		
Semi-circle – seats only		

I my last session I used:
I found it to be: satisfactory/unsatisfactory

Because:

When I teach again I will try:
Because:

We have reviewed the process of objective setting, cognitive learning and Socratic questioning techniques. We have also included a scrutiny of appropriate room arrangements, which is crucial in effective learning and teaching. In all, we hope that this chapter has proved useful in helping to reflect on your own practice, particularly planning and delivery, and that the case studies and tasks have provided some useful thoughts and suggestions for you to implement in the classroom.

Note

1 Inductive learning techniques imply an approach which encourages learners to produce the content of the session through carefully planned activities. Heuristic learning is about learners being given opportunities to 'discover' knowledge for themselves.

Further reading

Curzon, L.B. (1990) *Teaching in FE*, 4th edn. London: Cassell.

Dewey, J. (1938) *Experience and Education*. New York: Collier Macmillan.

Gill, D. and Adams, B. (1989) *ABC of Communication Studies*. London: Macmillan.

Knowles, M. (1980) *The Modern Practice of Adult Education: From Pedagogy to Andragogy*. Chicago, IL: Follett.

Knowles, M. (1984) *The Adult Learner: A Neglected Species*, 3rd edn. Houston, TX: Gulf Publishing Company.

Lefrancois, G.R. (1994) *Psychology for Teaching*, 8th edn. Belmont, CA: Wadsworth.

Tredway, L. (1995) Socratic seminars: engaging learners in intellectual discourse. *Educational Leadership* 53(1): 26–9.

4   Enabling students to learn

What is this chapter about?

This chapter looks at enabling students to learn in the 14–19 sector. It is important to ensure that young people master the basics of learning, for themselves, their employers and for us as tutors. Being aware of the different techniques that can be used with 14–19-year-old learners and how to create expert learners who are fully engaged in vocational education is the key to successful teaching with this age range. We consider how to analyse learners' specific needs and how to create expert learners who are independent and motivated to learn. We then look at accelerated learning, higher order thinking and emotional intelligence and consider transformational learning and the impact of this on learners.

Task 4.1 Preliminary reading

Duckworth, V., Wood, J., Dickinson, J. and Bostock, J. (2010) *Successful Teaching Practice in the Lifelong Learning Sector.* Exeter: Learning Matters.

Task 4.2

Consider your own learning and list the key things that help you to learn – why do you think they help you?

Learners' needs analysis

As Winston Churchill famously said 'I am always ready to learn although I do not always like being taught'. Yet courses are often designed, and even implemented, without any reference to the learners who take them.

This is almost never satisfactory, and can be a disaster, especially for 14–19 courses. The knowledge, abilities, skills, experience, preferences, attitudes and expectations of course participants should have a bearing on any course designed for them. After all no doctor prescribes medicine without a consultation and diagnosis. But how can the course designer develop a profile of the learners? This process is usually carried out very early in the course, or even before the course begins.

One way of discovering your learners' needs is to ask them to complete a questionnaire designed to discover the extent of their previous knowledge, experience, attitudes and expectations. You may like to include questions in the following areas. The examples that follow are for learners about to start an improvers' French class; for those beginning a course on the use of a sales computer system; and for those about to start an A level science course in a new college.

Knowledge
Do you know the French for glass, soup and lorry?
Do you know the company's complaints procedure?
Could you define molar concentration?

Skills and abilities
Could you translate the following letter?
Are you able to make use of the computer's back-up procedure?
Could you prepare a microscope slide to view a … ?

Experience
Have you ever read a French novel?
Have you ever used a computer before?
Have you used computers in the laboratory to measure temperature?

Attitudes and expectations
How many hours of set reading are you prepared to do per week?
What is your main reason for enrolling on this course?
Are you used to weekly homework?

Preferred learning styles
Do you enjoy reading round the class?
Would you like informal tests?
Which of the following do you enjoy: working in groups, … ?

Of course, such questions can be asked informally during discussion or during one-to-one conversation, but an anonymous questionnaire is likely to produce a more honest and representative learner profile. Another approach is to give learners a 'can do' questionnaire. The new learners are asked questions designed to obtain detailed information about their knowledge and skills. For example:

For a maths course:
Could you solve the following equation? $2x + 4x = 3x - 72$
Yes   I think so   No

For a health studies course:
Does diabetes require dietary management?
Yes   I think so   No

Twenty or so well-chosen questions like this will give you a detailed impression of your learners' prior learning. Learners can then be shown how to make good any individual deficiencies discovered by the questionnaire.

In addition to such course-specific screening tests, nearly all further education colleges in the UK routinely give all their full-time learners a screening test in basic numeracy and literacy. Learners may also be screened for study skills, attitudes to learning, and preferred learning styles and teaching methods. There will also be an attempt to discover any additional needs caused by impaired sight or hearing, mobility problems, medical conditions such as asthma or eczema, and other relevant physical factors. Emotional, behavioural or mental health factors can also mean that some learners will have particular needs.

How are all these needs to be met? Ideally each learner should have their individual needs diagnosed and an individual action plan negotiated and formulated. The course can then be adapted, and the learner can be shown how to make use of cross-college or school specialist support to meet their needs. They may need 'learning support' to help them with assignments, and to improve their numeracy or literacy. They may need specialist equipment, disability guidance, alternative arrangements for their course assessment, counselling or tutorial support. They may also need a catch-up programme of extra assignments, learning support, extra classes, or extra qualifications to make up for deficiencies in their prior learning, or to meet their career aspirations.

Learners need to know that the college is there to support them, whatever their needs or difficulties. But usually, they also need to take responsibility for making their own best use of this support. They need to be active rather than passive. This will require careful and sensitive monitoring by their tutors, who need to discover and celebrate learner successes, and help their learners to self-evaluate and set themselves attainable targets.

Meeting learner needs

There is an increasing expectation (see for example the Tomlinson Report) that colleges and courses should adapt to the learner, not the other way round. Modern educational philosophy makes great demands on colleges and schools. For example schools and colleges are expected to be responsive and adapt to student needs rather than regarding them as 'deficient'. Courses must be designed with student need in mind rather than allowing a 'sink or swim' attitude or an over-reliance on 'bolt-on' support. But this is also demanding of the learner.

Once learner needs have been discovered, you may find that it is necessary to split the class into groups engaged in different activities, in order to meet their disparate needs. You should also (formally or informally) discover whether you are meeting the needs of each individual learner. You could use a questionnaire but a one-to-one conversation after the first few course meetings might be better: 'Is the course as you expected?'; 'Is it too difficult or too easy?'; 'Are you enjoying the activities?'; 'Are the handouts detailed enough?'

Task 4.3

Thinking about your own practice, prepare a 'can do' questionnaire for one of your groups and see if it works. If so, consider how you could develop this further in the future.

Creating expert learners

Every learner needs to feel in control of, and take responsibility for, their own learning. This means every learner developing some expert learner characteristics. The ability to motivate ourselves to learn and to understand how to plan and manage learning most effectively to meet our goals is a significant expert learner characteristic. Teachers, trainers and managers are seeking ways to help learners and themselves learn how to learn.

Assessment for learning (AfL) is about generating and reflecting on the evidence of learning. It is a process in which learners and teachers together set learning goals, share learning intentions and success criteria and evaluate progress through learning conversations and self and peer assessment. Assessment for learning is the process of seeking and interpreting evidence that helps tutors to assess their learners' progress and helps learners to monitor themselves. The evidence will show where learners are in their learning and helps teachers and learners jointly to decide what the next steps should be.

AfL focuses attention on the 'how' of learning as well as the 'what' and is one of the most powerful ways of improving learning and raising standards. Building it into sessions means that learners understand:

- the goals they are pursuing;
- the criteria that will be applied to assessing their work;
- how they will receive feedback;
- how they will take part in assessing their learning;
- how they can make further progress.

This helps learners become more aware of how they learn and what they need to do in order to progress further.

Assessment for learning is a key tool in helping students become expert learners who demonstrate the following skills and characteristics:

1   an ability to recognize their own barriers to learning;
2   strategies to overcome barriers to learning;
3   self-belief, self-confidence, self-esteem;
4   organizational skills;
5   time management;
6   a developing range of learning styles and strategies;
7   attitudes, approaches and self-belief;
8   concentration;
9   'study skills', for example reading, essays, note taking;
10   listening skills;
11   revision skills;
12   success in exams;
13   being forward focused;
14   proficiency in action planning – setting SMART targets, reviewing, monitoring, evaluating;
15   understanding own values and goals;
16   memory skills;
17   locating and selecting resources;
18   processing information;
19   enquiry;
20   managing personal relationships;
21   awareness of strengths and weaknesses.

In developing expert learners, students may face obstacles or barriers to learning. An obstacle can be defined as something you see when you take your eyes off the goal, or things that hold us back or even excuses or reasons for not trying. When faced with an obstacle we have three choices: dealing with it in order to remove it; finding another way; or ignoring it and carrying on towards the goal.

So how can we help students become better learners?

- use language of choice;
- give students the opportunity to make choices;
- encourage and develop decision-making processes and skills;
- use praise;
- recognize achievements – even small ones;
- promote risk-taking in thinking and learning;
- use problem-solving approaches;
- communicate in adult mode;
- be future-focused.

Task 4.4

Visit the excellence gateway and have a look at their staff development activities on creating expert learners: www.excellencegateway.org.uk

Case study 4.1: Lorraine

My college serves communities which include the top 20 per cent most deprived districts in the country and are typified by poor levels of literacy and numeracy at all ages and unemployment rates of well above the national average. The college is a medium-sized further education establishment, with three main sites seeking to offer a range of vocational and academic courses, and work-based training.

Many students come to the college with low levels of attainment yet make excellent progress on courses and in their personal development, resulting in progression to higher education or into the working environment.

The atmosphere within the campus, where Art and Design is situated, has a 'family' feel. It is warm and welcoming, where each student is valued and encouraged to achieve their maximum potential through the patience and professional approach of the teachers. Every student is precious, with even the most challenging of learners nurtured and valued through provision of support for individual needs.

The Introductory Diploma in Art and Design course includes learners with behavioural issues, short attention span and lack of concentration, which may occasionally result in refusal to complete activities. Short-term targets are required and, for some, a lot of one-to-one support due to negativity about work and difficulty in remembering instructions. Encouragement and

(continued)

prompting with a range of practical activities helps to keep the group focused. LSA and dyslexia support are in place for most sessions but not within textiles lessons. Despite this the group has performed extremely well this year, responding to tasks in a positive manner and offering one another strong support, resulting in group cohesion and visible improvement in achievement and behaviour.

During a discussion about what works for them during lessons the conversation started as task orientated and rapidly moved to that of the home environment, which must also be considered: volunteers from this cohort who chose to give comments include individuals with barriers to learning and low attention span.

Paul commented that he particularly enjoys practical work, preferring to have techniques and processes demonstrated so that he has a full understanding of what is required from the end result. He, like the remainder of the cohort, has an aversion to written work; a mandatory requirement within the course via self reflection and evaluation of own work and description of techniques and processes used. Paul is a good communicator during discussion but finds it hard to put his thoughts into words at times and struggles more to do so when on paper.

Jack was of a similar opinion on practical work. He also said that he much prefers demonstration rather than explanation at all stages within the process, in order to gain full understanding of each stage and end stage result. Jack is partially sighted and another highly creative member of the group. His communication skills are excellent for the level of course that he attends, and he has a clear vision of taking a path towards study at university.

Lloyd wanted to comment on the use of objectives within sessions. Interestingly, although deemed good practice within the teaching profession, the use of objectives made no sense to Lloyd at all, begging the question 'For whose purpose are objectives meant to be addressed?' If they don't make sense to some of the learners then even the most SMART objectives written in a language that learners may understand are still useless.

Lloyd suggested that picture diagrams of the tasks are easier to understand, stating that if objectives must be used then they need to be teamed with an example of the task or a picture of what the end result should be. This observation underpins the fact that visuals provide strong support for certain learners.

Lloyd is a conscientious worker who remains on task but is not a fan of the competitive quiz on Monday mornings, which is when he had this group for their textiles lesson. Matt is a quieter member of the group who seems to have thrived within the social bond of this cohort yet, like most, finds it difficult to put his thoughts into words or writing. He said that he likes to work in groups and when working alone he prefers to listen to his music as it helps him to concentrate more effectively.

Rachel agreed with Matt and said that using her iPod helps to drown out everybody else in the room and to focus. This is a common theme within the group; some find it very difficult if the noise level starts to rise and become agitated if they cannot concentrate properly. Rachel is a quiet, diligent worker whose progress may go unnoticed within a cohort where the more attention-seeking members may take over and monopolize teacher activity. It is important to be aware of the activity of the whole of the class to ensure that support is offered to every learner. Rachel does not find the written work as much of a challenge as the remainder of the cohort but may feel a little on the spot during question and answer sessions.

Adam is a lively character who likes to sing within sessions and is drawn by the social aspects within class. When focused his comments can be extremely insightful and he is eager to participate in discussions to gain better understanding of topics. He said, 'It depends on the background noise and what's happening at home and outside college. If somebody you know is in hospital you aren't thinking about the work.'

Jack added, 'You have to know the student. If they have a rough background in their personal life they will do less than others sometimes. The teacher needs to communicate with the student to understand how they were at school and how they are. Talk to them and they will tell you their problems.'

Adam replied, 'It's not always about the classroom, it's things outside as well.'

Paul said that 'the teacher should ask how you are when you come into the lesson', to which Jack added, 'Always talk to the students equally. Don't leave anybody out. If a teacher is in a bad mood don't take it out on the students. Its ok for them to have a bad day but teachers need to try to keep their personal lives and moods to themselves, stay positive throughout their teaching hours when they are by themselves. Keep a positive attitude.'

The discussion turned to how friendly teachers are towards them and how it affects their behaviour in return. The group was in agreement that the more 'friendly' teachers often ask how they are and chat to them, occasionally joining in their conversations. On being allowed to chat within sessions Lloyd commented 'we finished on task but talked a lot. We still got the work done.'

Adam agreed, 'Sometimes we talk but sometimes we are talking about the work.'

(*continued*)

A sound piece of advice imparted from my mentor is 'We are not here to make friends'. At the time this seemed a little callous but I am now able to read between the lines. Learners begin to assess the teacher's non-verbal language from the outset and throw down challenges to test the waters. It can be a common mistake for new teachers to want to be 'friends' with their class.

Standing up to teach your first few sessions can be difficult enough without feeling that the cohort have an extreme dislike of you. Young adult learners are looking to be led; they need and are used to having a figure of authority. It makes them feel comfortable and safe. Providing a safe environment where all are valued is offering a space in which they can grow, away from the distractions of the outside world. This is particularly true for learners with barriers and particular needs. Stability, routine and structure have been a large part of my improvement in managing learners with needs who may become difficult if a task is too long or lacking in challenge.

Without the provision of an inclusive environment for all we would be failing learners who have already experienced failure of traditional schooling to engage them in their own development. For the cohort and teacher, where a strong cohesion and understanding is developed, there need be no boundaries to expansion of vocabulary or recollection of knowledge. These learners are waiting to be unlocked through structured and well-managed tasks with clearly defined outcomes in a positive environment where they are free of any labels which they may have been assigned during the school years.

Accelerated learning

When we 'learn' in ordinary situations (with a book or a teacher), we are actually using less than 20 per cent of our brain's capacity. Our learning potential isn't fixed. Intelligence is a group of abilities that can be developed. Accelerated learning, also known as 'super-learning' or 'brain-friendly learning', is a system designed to help people of all ages learn more and retain more by using the whole of the brain.

Accelerated learning increases your ability to learn by stimulating your brain to work harder. This can be done by creating new practical learning situations such as using drama to learn about science. If it's done as a group activity, the experience can be fun and rewarding.

For instance, at school students could build a giant floor model of a complex chemical compound, or create a one-minute drama about the life cycle of an insect or a key moment in history. Instead of simply writing about it, students might write a rap song about a complex geographical process. Such experiences will be memorable, so more will be learnt – and that will increase the desire for more learning.

Another important aspect of accelerated learning methods is to review new knowledge during the learning process. Studies show that the human brain forgets much of the information it processes during one day if that information isn't reviewed. To help your students remember what they have learnt, encourage them to talk about the main points each day. At the end of each week, get your class to review the main points again. They will be a step ahead when they come to revise for exams or assessments, too.

Learning by doing

Since we learn to talk by talking, swim by swimming and drive by driving, it makes sense to make learning anything as practical and activity based as possible. Working collaboratively (in a group) is ideal, because a learning 'community' will have more success than a collection of isolated individuals.

Left-brain and right-brain thinking

Traditional methods of learning concentrate on the left side of the brain (which controls our powers of language, logic and sequencing) more than the right side (which deals with forms and patterns, rhythm, space and imagination). Creating connections between both sides when we learn stimulates electrical-chemical impulses so that our 100 billion active brain cells work harder. We can learn many things simultaneously like the tune, rhythm and words to a song. This demonstrates that learning is not confined to one part of the brain, but can happen in both parts at once.

Left-brain learners prefer:

1. a step by step approach;
2. working in small steps up to the big picture;
3. a narrow focus;
4. dealing with steps in order and in isolation;
5. rules and structure;
6. logic rather than intuition;
7. facts rather than own experience.

Right-brain learners prefer:

1. to see 'the big picture' with a clear meaning and purpose;
2. working from the big picture down to the detail;

3   to explore in a personalized, intuitive way;
4   to jump in anywhere;
5   to avoid rules, structures and details;
6   making links and relations between topics and seeing patterns.

Nearly all tutors use some right-brain teaching strategies, but very few use them enough. Many activities do not take a great deal of time, and yet are very powerful as they help students to consolidate and structure their learning. The methods in Box 4.1 are particularly useful for learners who have not learned well with conventional methods, or who need a new approach. Many also challenge the most able.

Box 4.1   Examples of right-brain techniques

1   Mind maps, especially when used to summarize a topic. Learners' attempts are relatively easily improved after they have compared theirs with a model mind map provided by you. Learners can present their maps to each other or the class. (See section on mind maps below.)

2   Images, pictures, photographs, posters, diagrams, shapes and patterns, drawings, cartoons, graphs, charts, symbols, icons, logos, leaflets, etc. which make useful or important points. (Their value is in their power to explain, persuade and affect and so on.)

3   'Time lines' that show the development of something with time pictorially.

4   Colour coding for related but different concepts for example for handouts or projected images. Students' folders can be labelled or indexed using coloured card or paper, sticky coloured blobs, or icons.

5   Colour for impact.

6   DVD and CD Rom images.

7   Models and the real thing.

8   Visually interesting websites, animations, computer simulations and other computer visuals. PowerPoint presentations that are not too text dependent.

Whole-brain learning

With its emphasis on verbal skills, logic, efficiency, time management and linear thinking, the industrial era of recent Western history can be viewed as a left-brain dominated society. In contrast, the preceding agricultural era was largely a right-brain society with its emphasis on living with and by nature and the importance of social and familial relationships, spirituality and magic. The current knowledge and information era is going to require a whole-brain society. 'Hi-tech' will need to be balanced by 'Hi-touch'. Spiritual and social values need to develop alongside the extraordinary technological advances now occurring at an exponential growth rate.

Not surprisingly, the curriculum of our schools and colleges has been primarily left-brain dominated with the emphasis on reading, writing and arithmetic. Talking has been discouraged. Learning has been by rote or by taking notes or listening, not by active involvement, discussion and experiment. This has presented some problems for students who prefer right-brain learning; think, for example, about these teacher statements, which have been heard in classrooms:

'Stop chatting, you won't learn anything while you're talking!'
But a right-brainer often learns best while he/she *is* talking.

'Stop fidgeting and concentrate on your work.'
But a right-brainer *is* probably concentrating while he/she is fidgeting. He/she will need to move about the classroom, and will often like to work part-way out of his/her seat or standing up.

'You won't find the answer on the ceiling.'
But a right-brainer is visual and probably will. He/she will be spelling out a word, or visualizing a page with the answer on it, or picturing a solution.

'Stop chewing your pencil and get on with your work.'
Right-brainers typically chew pencils, doodle, wander back and forth to the pencil sharpener, chew their tongues, and make faces while they work.

'How can you work at a desk as messy as that?'
Left-brainers often have very tidy desks. Right-brainers' minds do not operate in such a sequential, structured, ordered way and their desks tend to reflect this.

'You never get your work in on time.'
Right-brainers will often have real difficulty with time keeping. The existing school structure is not kind to such people and they will need help to fit into a way of life which to them is unnatural.

'That's a stupid answer.'

But is it? Right-brainers will often see connections and relate ideas together in unpredictable ways. A left-brainer may simply interpret it as the wrong answer.

'Don't ask so many questions.'

But a right-brainer can hardly stop himself/herself, because he/she will tend to think of more questions than the average left-brainer.

'It's no good getting the right answer if you don't know how you got it.'

Right-brainers use intuition and gut reaction. Sometimes an answer 'feels right' or just pops into their heads. They find it difficult to explain the process because it is not logical. They 'know' that $1/4$ is less than $1/2$ but cannot explain why. They sometimes are accused of cheating because of this.

'Why don't you read the instructions before launching into the question or exam?'

Right-brainers get bored reading lines in sequence and want to get on with the task. While we still have the present examination format they will need considerable help with this.

'Don't argue. That is the way it is and that is the way it has to be.'

Left-brainers deal with the way things are. They are more likely to accept reality.

Task 4.5

We would like to believe that such statements would not be as 'typical' today as they were, say, in the 1980s. What do you think? Have you heard similar in your practice?

Mind mapping

Mind mapping is a very effective learning strategy. Our memories work by creating a network of patterns of associated ideas. A mind map can imitate this pattern and so the brain can relate to the information more easily. Mind maps can be used in a variety of ways, for example to review the previous lesson or to summarize information and ideas. They are also helpful in presenting information to give the overall structure of a topic as well as bringing together information from different sources and helping learners think through complex problems. (You might want to visit www.thinkbuzan.com, the official website of Tony Buzan who invented mind mapping.)

The advantages of mind mapping include the following:

1 The main theme is in the centre and is therefore more clearly defined.
2 The relative importance of each idea is clearly indicated – more important ideas are near the centre.
3 Words linked to pictures can be remembered easily and engage both sides of the brain.
4 Meaning is vital to memory and mind maps develop understanding and meaning between topics.
5 Mind mapping gives an overview – the big picture.
6 The use of pictures and drawings encourages creativity and engages both sides of the brain – pictures are remembered more easily than words.

Mind mapping expands thinking skills by developing:

1 information-processing skills;
2 reasoning skills;
3 enquiry skills;
4 creative thinking skills;
5 evaluative skills.

When starting a mind map with students you should ensure you always put the main theme in the centre of the mind map and signpost the branches you want them to draw, making the sub-themes. Try to use single key words for each concept and suggest pictures/symbols for each concept.

Checking learning

In order to check learning:

1 Start and end the lesson with a recap activity to check that learning has been retained.
2 Throughout the session check that learning has taken place at the end of each activity.
3 If you are using Q&A use a variety of questioning techniques:
   Which?   Questions for evaluation.
   How?   Questions for synthesis.

Why?	Questions for analysis.
Open questions	To elicit a general response.
Directed questions	To check specific students' understanding.

4   If an observer comes into the lesson part way through, find an opportunity to pull the group together, recap and check learning and then allow them to carry on.

5   You need to be able to show that every student has learnt during the lesson – they may have learnt different things but they should ALL have made progress towards their learning goal.

6   Try to vary your methods for checking learning – do not rely on Q&A only as it may not show the true extent to which learning has taken place as some students may be visual learners, auditory learners or kinaesthetic learners.

7   The emphasis should be on the students' learning experience and not what you have taught.

Higher order thinking skills and Bloom's taxonomy

Higher order thinking by students involves the transformation of information and ideas. This transformation occurs when students combine facts and ideas and synthesize, generalize, explain, hypothesize or arrive at some conclusion or interpretation. Manipulating information and ideas through these processes allows students to solve problems, gain understanding and discover new meaning.

When students engage in the construction of knowledge, an element of uncertainty is introduced into the instructional process and the outcomes are not always predictable. In other words, the teacher is not certain what the students will produce. In helping students become producers of knowledge, the teacher's main instructional task is to create activities or environments that allow them opportunities to engage in higher order thinking.

Bloom's taxonomy is a classification of thinking organized by level of complexity. It gives teachers and students an opportunity to learn and practise a range of thinking and provides a simple structure for many different kinds of questions and thinking.

Bloom's revised taxonomy

Blooms taxonomy recognizes six levels of thinking skills, divided into two categories, higher order and lower order, as detailed in Box 4.2.

Box 4.2

Higher order thinking skills:
Creating
Generating new ideas, products, or ways of viewing things
Designing, constructing, planning, producing, inventing

Evaluating
Justifying a decision or course of action
Checking, hypothesizing, critiquing, experimenting, judging

Analysing
Breaking information into parts to explore understandings and relationships
Comparing, organizing, deconstructing, interrogating, finding

Lower order thinking skills:
Applying
Using information in another familiar situation
Implementing, carrying out, using, executing

Understanding
Explaining ideas or concepts
Interpreting, summarizing, paraphrasing, classifying, explaining

Remembering
Recalling information
Recognizing, listing, describing, retrieving, naming, finding

Using Bloom's taxonomy to question learners

The taxonomy involves all categories of questions. Typically a teacher would vary the level of questions within a single lesson. Lower level questions are those at the remembering, understanding and lower level application levels of the taxonomy. Usually questions at the lower levels are appropriate for evaluating students' preparation and comprehension; diagnosing students' strengths and weaknesses and reviewing and/or summarizing content. Higher level questions are those requiring complex application, analysis, evaluation or creation skills. Questions at higher levels of the taxonomy are usually most appropriate for encouraging students to think more deeply and critically; for problem solving; encouraging discussions and stimulating students to seek information on their own.

Examples of lower order questions

1 What happened after . . . ?
2 How many . . . ?
3 What is . . . ?
4 Who was it that . . . ?
5 Can you name . . . ?
6 Find the definition of . . .
7 Describe what happened after . . .
8 Who spoke to . . . ?
9 Which is true or false . . . ?
10 Can you explain why . . . ?
11 Can you write in your own words . . . ?
12 How would you explain . . . ?
13 Can you write a brief outline . . . ?
14 What do you think could have happened next . . . ?
15 Who do you think . . . ?
16 What was the main idea . . . ?
17 Can you clarify . . . ?
18 Can you illustrate . . . ?
19 Do you know of another instance where . . . ?
20 Can you group by characteristics such as . . . ?
21 Which factors would you change if . . . ?
22 What questions would you ask of . . . ?
23 From the information given, can you develop a set of instructions about . . . ?

Examples of higher order questions

1 How is . . . similar to . . . ?
2 What do you see as other possible outcomes?
3 Why did . . . changes occur?
4 Can you explain what must have happened when . . . ?
5 What are some of the problems of . . . ?
6 Can you distinguish between . . . ?
7 What were some of the motives behind . . . ?
8 What was the turning point?
9 What was the problem with . . . ?
10 Is there a better solution to . . . ?
11 Judge the value of . . . What do you think about . . . ?
12 Can you defend your position about . . . ?
13 Do you think . . . is a good or bad thing?
14 How would you have handled . . . ?

15   What changes to ... would you recommend?
16   Do you believe ... ? How would you feel if ... ?
17   How effective are ... ?
18   What are the consequences ... ?
19   What influence will ... have on our lives?
20   What are the pros and cons of ... ?
21   Why is ... of value?
22   What are the alternatives?
23   Who will gain and who will lose?
24   Can you design a ... to ... ?
25   Can you see a possible solution to ... ?
26   If you had access to all resources, how would you deal with ... ?
27   Why don't you devise your own way to ... ?
28   What would happen if ... ?
29   How many ways can you ... ?
30   Can you create new and unusual uses for ... ?
31   Can you develop a proposal which would ... ?

Task 4.6

Use a range of these higher order questions in your next lesson and monitor the quality of the answers you receive. Do they engage the learners in higher order thinking?

Emotional intelligence

Emotions in everyday learning are vital to the well-being of individuals and communities. Emotional intelligence is the ability to understand our emotions and to learn from them, to use them to our advantage and to understand and empathize with others and their emotions. One of the basic emotional skills that 14–19-year-olds need to develop involves being able to recognize feelings and put a name to them. It is also important to be aware of the relationship between thoughts, feelings and actions. What thought sparked off that feeling? What feeling was behind that action?

It is important to realize what is behind feelings. Beliefs have a fundamental effect on the ability to act and on how things are done. Many people continually give themselves negative messages. Hope can be a useful asset. In addition, finding ways for 14–19-year-olds to deal with anger, fear, anxiety and sadness is essential: learning how to soothe oneself when upset, for example. One can learn to understand what happens when emotions get the upper hand, and how to gain time to judge if what is about to be said or done in the heat of the moment is really the best thing to do. Being able to channel emotions to a positive end is a key aptitude.

Getting the measure of a situation and being able to act appropriately requires understanding the feelings of the others involved and being able to empathize with their perspective. It is important to be able to listen to them without being carried away by personal emotions. There's a need to be able to distinguish between what others do or say, and personal reactions and judgements.

Developing quality relationships has a very positive effect on all involved. What feelings are being communicated to others? Enthusiasm and optimism are contagious as are pessimism and negativity. Being able to express personal concerns without anger or passivity is a key asset.

For young people to know how and when to take the lead and when to follow is essential for effective cooperation. Effective leadership is not built on domination but on the art of helping people work together on common goals. Recognizing the value of the contribution of others and encouraging their participation can often do more good than giving orders or complaining. At the same time, there is a need to take responsibility, recognize the consequences of decisions and acts, and follow through on commitments.

In resolving conflicts there is a need to understand the mechanisms at work. Young people in conflict are generally locked into a self-perpetuating emotional spiral in which the declared subject of conflict is rarely the key issue. Much conflict resolution calls on using other emotional skills (see Box 4.3).

Box 4.3

Young people need to develop the following attributes:

1 being able to motivate oneself;
2 persistence in the face of frustrations;
3 control of impulses;
4 delaying gratification;
5 ability to regulate one's moods;
6 being able to keep distress from swamping the ability to think;
7 being able to empathize;
8 recognizing one's own emotions;
9 managing emotions;

10   recognizing emotions in others;
11   handling relationships;
12   observing themselves and recognizing their feelings;
13   knowing the relationship between thoughts, feelings and reactions;
14   examining their actions and knowing their consequences;
15   knowing if thought or feeling is ruling a decision;
16   identifying what is behind feelings;
17   finding ways to handle fear, anxiety and anger;
18   learning the value of exercise, relaxation methods, and so on;
19   understanding others' feelings and concerns and taking their perspective;
20   appreciating the differences in how people feel about things;
21   talking about feelings effectively;
22   becoming a good listener and question-asker;
23   valuing openness and building trust in a relationship;
24   knowing when it is safe to risk talking about their private feelings;
25   identifying patterns in their emotional life and reactions;
26   recognizing similar patterns in others;
27   feeling pride and seeing themselves in a positive light;
28   recognizing their strengths and weaknesses;
29   being able to laugh at themselves;
30   accepting their feelings and moods;
31   following through on commitments.

Task 4.7

Think about a recent situation in which a young person has shown behavioural issues in your classroom. Could you have dealt with it better using emotional intelligence? Could they?

Transformational learning

In education, and in many other situations, people often do not learn what they could learn or what they are supposed to learn. This is something that can affect young learners who have not done well at school as they often have defence mechanisms that preclude them from learning.

These can be caused by many factors including a poor experience of education in previous situations.

A Danish professor, Knud Illeris, talks about how we control our learning:

> Through everyday consciousness we control our own learning and non-learning in a manner that seldom involves any direct positioning while simultaneously involving a massive defence of the already acquired understandings and, in the final analysis, our very identity.
>
> (Illeris 2009: 15)

This can result in people finding it very hard to learn new concepts. Without what Kegan (2009) refers to as 'transformational learning' they may struggle with the whole process. Transformational learning is advocated by Robert Kegan who explains that every learner comes with a 'learning past' and that this is an important part of their present and future learning. Important features of this past, especially for disaffected learners, are their history of the subject at hand and their personal disposition towards learning itself (Kegan 2009: 45). As educators we need to be aware of learners' learning pasts and their histories of prior transformations in order to decide which strategies to use to support their current learning. This is central to our role and informs many of the strategies we need to employ. If learners have previously undergone a form of transformational learning they are far more likely to do the same again to adapt to the new demands of the current situation.

14–19-year-old learners may already have certain well-developed ideas about life in line with their own systems and beliefs. To admit that they need to learn something new is to admit there is something incomplete with their present knowledge base. Many of these learners, though they may perceive that they do need new skills or knowledge, feel so threatened by the challenge to their previous beliefs that they are unable to learn (Rogers 2007).

Of course, if this is the case it is difficult for them to change their existing patterns of behaviour. Change is at the heart of learning. If nothing changes then there is no learning. But essentially we will only change when what we want presents itself as a bigger reward than the cost of staying the same, so dissatisfaction is a great motivator (Rogers 2007).

14–19-year-old learners may not have been fully engaged in their education for a number of years, but they will still have learnt a great deal. Their learning, especially of practical things, will have been gained 'by doing'. They will have solved problems and handled issues by discovering solutions through discovery, trial and error and proven success. However, these young people can lack confidence in themselves as learners, often underestimating their own powers and potential. They tend to be over-anxious and reluctant to risk making mistakes. Above all they will not want to fail and look foolish.

Jack Mezirow originally developed the theory of transformational learning in the 1970s. Transformational learning claims that when individuals engage in critical reflection they reach deeper understandings of their own personal experiences and are able to use this to develop new perspectives on education and to re-engage with education on a different level. Mezirow states that: 'Transformations may be epochal – sudden major reorientations in habit of mind, often associated with significant life crises – or cumulative, a progressive sequence of insights resulting in changes of point of view and leading to transformation in habit of mind' (Mezirow 2009: 94).

This concept of transformational learning is fundamental to understanding our learners and where they are placed in their own learning journeys. Some learners will have undergone some form of transformation and will have a readiness to learn and some will not yet have undertaken the self-reflection necessary to transform their own view of learning and may definitely not have a readiness to learn. This is particularly evident when the course of study being undertaken is not embarked upon willingly but is a necessary part of their schooling.

Transitions are periods of change in our lives that seem to alternate with periods of stability. Transitional periods are inevitable in the lives of all young people and can lead to a questioning of the formerly stable, solid foundations of a person's life.

Most 14–19-year-olds in education are going through a transition period in their lives, particularly those undertaking vocational training and preparing to enter a specific career. This can be very challenging and can cause a negative reaction to those providing the teaching. On the other hand there can be an embracing of the new learning and opportunities opening up. This depends on the nature of the transition and the extent of the learner's choice in that transitional process.

We need to link participation to the quality of the experience. Participating on its own is not sufficient to empower and enable learners to achieve. They must be able to enjoy the experience and gain emotional and academic benefits from it as Rogers observes: 'Learning should involve the student as a whole person; at an emotional and personal as well as at an intellectual level, learning should be pleasurable and relevant' (Rogers 1983: 20). Rogers clearly links these issues and talks about the student as a whole person and meeting their need for a pleasurable learning experience. It is the offering of opportunities to participate and the provision of the resources and materials to support the learners in that participation that will address the negative experiences of disadvantaged individuals and communities. As Race suggests: 'Learning is done by individuals; each learner learns in a particular way. Inclusive teaching is about helping all learners to optimize their own individual learning' (Race 2005: 157). Encouraging learners to engage actively in their learning and to enjoy the experience is part of the role of the tutor. Yet the responsibility and decision to engage and enjoy the learning is that of the learner. To that end, the point they are at in their learning journey and transformation must influence their receptiveness to the process of learning.

Case study 4.2: Axel

Axel is in his mid-40s and left school with a few CSEs at low grades. He joined the army and gained qualifications in carpentry and joinery, and crane driving. He was an explosives expert and did a level 3 apprenticeship. On leaving the army he worked as a carpenter for a number of firms until becoming a lecturer in carpentry and joinery two years ago.

Prior to starting this venture he had never studied an academic course but had enjoyed the teaching in the army. 'I enjoyed it in the army because it was different to school: At school I did not see the relevance of anything like that but when it was put towards something practical I could see the relevance.' He was unsure what to expect from the teaching course he was compelled to take, explaining 'I did not understand how it would help me to teach; it was just a piece of paper. So I had no real expectations of what it would do for me because obviously I had no prior knowledge of it and not much information from other people who had done it.'

He struggled with his first assignment saying: 'I thought what I had done was quite good, for me. It was very difficult and I wrote it about eight times and it was rubbish. But at the time I thought it was good.'

When asked how he feels about that work now he says: 'It was drivel, absolute drivel! I looked back on it during this last year and I actually corrected it, all the grammar and so on. I am still not great at it but I am a lot better than that now.'

Asked about the support he has received he says: 'I took all the support, I think. I am very eager to learn so if anybody offered me something I would take it. I knew if I needed any help it would be there. I asked everybody for help, you, my partner, my peers – I am a sponge, I like to get all views.'

He was then asked why he was a 'sponge' now and yet he wasn't at school. He replied: 'I have kids and I have made some mistakes in my life, and I see them and I know they are very bright and I'd like to be a role model for them. So when they see their dad as a teacher it might inspire them to do something else – to be as "up there" as a teacher. One of them wants to be a fighter pilot and he is passionate about that. So it's just so my lads have got a role model.'

We then went on to explore when he became a 'sponge'. He describes it as follows. 'It started before I started teaching. I came into teaching ready to learn even though there were certain members of staff who said "You will never do that. . . " so I did it to show I was better than them. They kept trying to put me down so I decided actually I am going to do it to be a role model to my kids.'

He is pleased with his academic journey so far saying, 'I am very very proud of myself, I must admit. I would be a liar if I said I wasn't. You know me, I am quite shy, but when I do something good I like to think "I did that" and I can honestly say I am proud of all the work I have done.'

When asked about how he has changed and what made him change he says, 'Things came together at the same time. My new partner, who is ambitious and academic, believed I could do more. My children were growing up and I wanted to be a role model to them and I started the course and realized I was capable of doing this. Anything I do I want to be the best at. I want to win all the time.'

He sums this up by saying, 'I learnt more by watching you, how you do it. I am a practical learner by trade, I learn by watching people do things. Watching you teach the theory by using practical techniques and activities helped me to see the links and to do the same in my teaching.' As we can see he has changed and is clear about his own motivations that enabled him to change.

So what does this mean for us as tutors in the 14–19 sector? By understanding the nature of transformational learning and being aware that all learners undergo transformations during their lives in relation to their learning, their ability to learn and their desire to learn, we can facilitate those transformations. To do this we need to allow opportunities for reflection and discussion about individuals' learning journeys and learning pasts. By reflecting on these experiences we can help them to move forward, to open up their minds to new learning opportunities and to awaken their will to learn.

Not all learners will go through this process at the same time or even at all during the programme you are delivering. But it is important to provide opportunities for them to undergo transformations in their approaches to learning in order to truly maximize their potential and to get the best out of them.

Chapter summary

This chapter has introduced some of the key concepts and ideas around understanding how students learn. One of the constant challenges that face tutors in the 14–19 sector is answering the question: 'How do we know how young people learn and how can we encourage that learning in our classrooms?' By considering ideas such as accelerated learning, emotional intelligence and transformational learning we begin to understand a little more about the motivations, thoughts and desires that drive young people. As a result we will be better placed to help them achieve their learning goals.

Further reading

Hughes, M. (2006) *And the Main Thing is Learning*. Cheltenham: Education and Training Support.

Race, P. (2005) *Making Learning Happen*. London: Sage.

Smith, A., Lovatt, M. and Wise, D. (2003) *Accelerated Learning: A User's Guide*. Stafford: Network Press.

5 Assessment methodology

What is this chapter about?

This chapter will purposefully re-visit PCET assessment methodology, with a view to examining its effectiveness in 14–16 transitions into PCET as well as the 14–19 age range. The chapter is structured in several sections and will first draw upon andragogical (adult learning) methods of teaching and learning to suggest assessment strategies which in turn value and support learners' achievements. Secondly, we review the notions of memory and cognition which will also give you ideas on structuring such strategies. Thirdly, there will be opportunities to sample a range of e-assessment methodologies. There are tasks and case studies to enable you to fully engage with and implement assessments which meet the needs of you and your learners.

Task 5.1 Preliminary reading

Tummons, J. (2007) *Achieving QTLS: Assessing Learning in the Life Long Learning Sector*, 2nd Edn. Exeter: Learning Matters Ltd.

Methods of assessment

We start by considering:

- What are the various methods of assessment?
- Which of them is appropriate for 14–19 learning and teaching?
- What strategies ensue from the various methods of assessment?

There are several recognized groups of assessment methods:

1 Formative assessment is often mistakenly thought to apply only at the start of a course or programme of study. In fact, a formative assessment may be useful at a number of stages during a programme of study.

Essentially, formative assessment is to do with diagnosis, guidance and action planning. This should always happen at the beginning of a course of study. Indeed, the funding mechanism applied to further education requires that this process takes place and is recorded for audit purposes. Learners and trainees will be assessed, offered guidance and have action plans formulated with them before they embark on a programme of learning.

However, formative assessment is a continuous process, which allows tutors and trainers to revisit the learners' progress and review all three phases (diagnosis, guidance and action planning) at other times during the programme. End of term reports are familiar to most of us from our school days – these are formative assessments. They are a means of re-assessing the learner and the programme of study. Tutors and trainers use formative assessment in an informal and casual way all the time. There will be occasions when this takes place as part of a formal process, often styled 'individual action planning'. At regular intervals the learner and the tutor or mentor will review progress and plan for the future. Most courses of study will incorporate some formal means of review as an integral part of full time programmes.

2 Summative assessment completes or 'sums up' a process or programme of study, as the title implies. Often it will mark the end of a course of study, the terminal examination, for example. Many of us have experienced final examinations – GCSEs, A Levels, the driving test, music and dance exams and many others. Of course a summative assessment does not have to take the form of an examination. Many of the newer programmes and certificates involve assessment of competence or knowledge at stages throughout the course, adding building blocks towards a final qualification. Some traditional programmes – the module A level for example – are structured in this way too.

3 Norm-referencing is a process applied to the end result of assessment to standardize and rank performance in relation to the highest and lowest level of attainment shown by other candidates. It may also compare performance with that of previous cohorts. The achievement of each individual is measured by comparing that person to the learner's particular class or group or even a wider group of candidates, such as the total annual cohort taking a particular subject. Referencing may be confined to one cohort, or to a range. If the 'norm' relies on the range and distribution of marks, for instance, then the 'standard' will not be fixed. It is self-evident that a range of 14 per cent to 87 per cent will result in a different 'norm' from a range of 28 per cent to 71 per cent.

Norm-referencing is designed to enable selection when there is competition for limited places at higher levels of education, employment or training and to enable examiners to rank learners in a particular cohort in order of preference. It is more likely to be used when demand for access exceeds places available and the criteria for excellent or exceptional candidates remain implicit whilst agencies or institutions wish to select quickly from the 'best' candidates available.

Norm-referencing may be based on predetermined criteria but these often rely on implicit notions of good/excellent/poor performance. They are not usually made explicit to learners and may not be very specific or consistent between examiners. Sometimes assessors are unaware of the implicit criteria that inform their judgements. The actual 'level' or 'standard' of achievement gained for the top and failure mark can also vary with each cohort. Information about rank order is more important to its users than details of individual achievements or how these were gained.

4 Criterion-referencing compares an individual's performance with specific, external and explicit criteria rather than with other learners' performance. A simple example would be reaching a qualifying time or distance in an athletics tournament. All those achieving the criterion should satisfy the judges – until that is other selection factors come into play! Criterion-referencing is designed to:

- provide specific information about what individuals actually can do;
- make requirements for assessment, differentiated grades and/or levels of 'mastery' or 'excellence' clearer to learners and assessors;
- enable assessors to differentiate on a simple pass/not yet passed basis;
- recognize a wide range of diversity among individuals rather than ranking them against the performance of others.

Criterion-referenced assessment is more likely to be used when there is a desire to remove barriers to access to education, training and employment by being explicit about what entry requirements are and when access or licence to practice requires a clearer and more detailed description of competence than is provided through descriptions of rank order.

5 Ipsative (or self) referencing is a form of criterion-referencing which measures a person's performance against their own previous performance and self-defined criteria. It can be used alongside other approaches since these criteria allow an individual learner to reach their own standard of achievement. In some programmes, however, it is sufficient on its own and other externally-defined criteria need not be used. The process can build up confidence and the skills of self-assessment before learners move on to measurement against externally defined standards.

Ipsative assessment is more likely to be used when:

- learners want to chart their own progress and set their own targets;
- assessment against an external standard is not appropriate or required;
- learners want or need to develop the ability to assess their own work independently of the tutor.

Assessment of this kind is commonly associated with sports performance and self-actualizing activities like Outward Bound courses, individual action planning and staff development. It is also commonplace in tutoring. However, it rarely surfaces as a public measure of performance in the way that examinations do.

Many qualifications and learning programmes use a combination of ipsative, criterion-referenced and norm-referenced assessment but the reasons for using these forms of assessment are not often made clear. Learners are often uncertain about what criteria are being used or how they relate to assessment methods or grading and marking systems. This can prevent learners from making the best use of their skills and previous experience. Many accreditation systems are based on criterion-referenced assessment and disassociate themselves from norm-referencing. However, underlying notions such as 'advanced', 'basic' and 'average' may involve an implicit use of norms.

An organization strategy for assessment enables tutors and assessors to share their expertise by being much more specific about different levels of performance (and making the criteria which underpin these explicit to learners). This enables learners to recognize what has been achieved and to set targets for improving performance. It also provides better descriptions of achievement and rank order to employers and admissions tutors.

Analysing the learning outcomes that underpin different levels of achievement reduces the tendency to use criteria that implicitly compare learners with each other and provides more information on their individual strengths and weaknesses. The effectiveness of assessment is therefore increased if organizations use an assessment strategy to examine:

- implicit criteria which might be used by assessors, admissions tutors and employers;
- reasons for using particular forms of assessment at different stages of learning programmes;
- how assessment methods relate to learning outcomes and how evidence of these outcomes will be provided for a range of interested parties;
- how results will be recorded and interpreted by different users;
- whether norm-referenced, criterion-referenced and ipsative assessment are being used appropriately in learning programmes.

Both formative and summative assessment use some form of criteria or standards for measurement. These may be explicitly or implicitly based on:

- general notions of how an excellent/average/poor learner performs (norm-referencing);
- direct comparisons with other learners in the same group or cohort (norm-referencing);
- an absolute, externally defined measure or standard (criterion-referencing);
- a learner's own previous performance (self-referencing or 'ipsative assessment').

There are different 'stages' and purposes of assessment. Each stage produces particular outcomes and information. The next section explores the effects of these outcomes on our beliefs about assessment.

Timing and purpose of assessment

You have probably identified most or all of the values and uses of assessment at different stages in a learning programme. Here are some of our ideas.

Assessment before the start of a session or course:

- should establish the prior knowledge and experience of your learners.

Assessment during the session or course:

- allows for checking that learners have understood a point before you attempt to build on it;
- enables the session or course to match the pace of the individual's or group's progress;
- facilitates the diagnosis of weaknesses to be overcome and strengths to be built on;
- enables you to revise your planned programme in the light of progress made and difficulties encountered.

Assessment at the end of the session or course:

- enables you to review the progress of the course and revise the programme, highlighting changes in presentation and organization for the future;
- may be necessary for learners to have their achievements certificated.

The outcomes of all types of assessment provide information about learners for them and for you. Failure to recognize the purposes of assessment can cause confusion and lead to conflicting views about why assessment is important, how and when it should be done and who should be involved.

Beliefs about assessment can become barriers to disseminating good practice, to developing assessors' skills and to recognizing and recording a broad range of achievements.

What is assessment for?

Assessment can be used for diagnostic purposes, for generating feedback for learners and for ensuring standards are met.

Diagnosis

- establish entry behaviour;
- diagnose learning needs/difficulties.

Feedback

- feedback to learners on their progress;
- diagnose strengths and areas for development;
- reinforce learning;
- feedback to tutors;
- motivate learners.

Standards

- maintain standards;
- certificate achievement;
- facilitate progression;
- predict future performance/selection;
- qualify as 'safe-to-practice', for example driving, nursing;
- data for Quality Assurance System.

Reasons for assessing learning

Assessment can:

- identify what specific knowledge or skills a learner wants or needs to acquire;

- establish how a learner could achieve the outcomes they are aiming for;
- motivate a learner to continue with a learning programme;
- justify awarding a qualification.

Assessment provides tutors with evidence that learning has taken place and valuable feedback for evaluating and improving their teaching methods. At the same time students gain feedback on their successes.

What are the main principles of assessment?

- validity: is the assessment the right assessment?
- reliability: will all assessors give the same judgement?
- manageability: is the assessment easily carried out?
- currency: is the assessment up to date and relevant?
- sufficiency: does the assessment assess an appropriate amount of learning?
- authenticity: is the assessment work that is submitted actually that of the learner involved?
- fairness: is the assessment non-biased and appropriate for the cohort?
- inclusiveness: are all learners able to be involved in the assessment?
- fitness for purpose: does the assessment measure what it is supposed to measure?

Task 5.2

Consider the six assessment situations listed below and comment on their:

- validity
- reliability
- sufficiency
- manageability
- authenticity
- fairness
- inclusiveness

If there are problems then consider what might be being assessed or how they might be assessed differently or additionally to meet the criteria.

1   In order to demonstrate knowledge of food hygiene learners are given a set of multiple-choice questions. They have to get 70 per cent correct answers to pass and obtain their certificate.

(continued)

2 To assess learners' knowledge of the colour wheel in Art and Design learners are asked to paint individually an object which makes use of that knowledge.

3 To assess their individual awareness of equal opportunities issues regarding race, a group is asked to take part in a discussion on the subject of trans-racial adoption. Their contributions and opinions will be observed by members of the group in turn and the discussions will be evaluated by everyone afterwards.

4 In order to assess their skills in using spoken English ESOL learners are asked to rate themselves on a scale of 1 (weak) to 10 (excellent).

5 In order to test their individual ability to work in a group, six adults are asked to organize and carry out a weekend camping expedition. A tutor will accompany the group and write a report afterwards matching their performance to agreed criteria.

6 To assess learners' understanding of the origins of the conflict in Iraq they are asked to write a 6,000 word essay.

Task 5.3

Consider one of your own assessment methods. Reflect personally on this or present it to your group. They will then question you on it to determine how well it meets the principles of assessment. Group members should consider themselves both as a learner being assessed in this way and as the tutor.

Choose one learning outcome from your teaching programme. Complete the information below:

- Who is involved in assessment?
- What is the method of assessment?
- When does the assessment take place?
- How is the assessment recorded?
- Comments:

Task 5.4

Having reflected on or discussed Task 5.3 continue with the following paired activity:

- Choose an assessment strategy you use.
- Identify what type of assessment it is.

- Analyse, through questioning your partner, if their assessment meets assessment principles.
- Identify what problems there might be and if they could be rectified.
- Be prepared to report back to the group on your discussions.

Task 5.5 is particularly useful in enabling you and your learners to grasp the concepts of weighting, validity and reliability and shows how crucial the role of assessor is in providing fair and just judgement on learners' efforts. You could use this task as a group of practitioners or as a classroom activity with your learners.

Task 5.5

Devise a system to judge which is the best of a number of supermarkets. Your response to this task will bring out some of the basic principles of assessment.

Now discuss the problems and issues that this exercise raises about the assessment process. For example, consider:

- Was the marking consistent . . . Why/why not?
- Was it fair?
- Would you have chosen the same assessment criteria as the assessors?
- Did the two different assessment types make a difference to how you performed the task? Any other difference?

The usual approach to assessment is to break down the overall task into more manageable parts, for example in the task above you might consider the following as important factors by which to judge a supermarket:

Prices
Variety of products
Customer care
Accessibility

These important factors are known as the *assessment criteria* against which you can judge each supermarket.

You might consider some assessment criteria to be more important than others. This is a matter of professional opinion and will often need a great deal of discussion. The relative importance of the criteria can be indicated by *weighting*. The group that put forward the assessment criteria below thought that price and accessibility were much more important than other factors.

> Prices (weighting 35 per cent)
> Variety of products (weighting 20 per cent)
> Customer care (weighting 15 per cent)
> Accessibility (weighting 30 per cent)

In this example a good score for prices would contribute more to the overall judgement than a good score for customer care.

You will need to make sure that all your judges have the same understanding of the criteria. A judge that thinks accessibility is all about car parks will give a different assessment to one who thinks it is a matter of opening times, hence the assessments would have a problem of *reliability*. A reliable assessment system is one where all trained assessors would give the same assessment to a particular candidate.

By giving a score to each of the criteria you would be able to declare a winner although people who didn't agree with your criteria or weighting would not agree with your final judgement; they would question the *validity* of your assessment (were you really judging the right things?).

Rather than making a judgement about which supermarket is best you might prefer to give a commentary against each assessment criterion. In this case the assessment can give a good description of the nature of each supermarket, without having to say that one is the winner and others are failures. This is often the most appropriate method of communicating assessments to learners since it is unlikely that you have the relatively simple task of deciding which is best.

Variables that could affect assessment include the subjective interpretation of the given criteria for assessment and the level of tutor involvement and intervention in the conduct of the assessment tasks. 'Rate' variables – the perception of the person making the assessment (filters) – and the circumstances and environment in which the assessment takes place are also likely to affect assessment.

Developing an assessment strategy

Every course needs an assessment strategy. This should be related to the aims and objectives for the course and should respond to considerations such as the following:

- What are the purposes of your assessment – to grade or to diagnose? (You may also assess to motivate, get feedback, acknowledge progress, certificate, select learners, evaluate courses, or some combination of these.)
- What is to be assessed? How is it to be done?
- Who will assess whom and when? Are marks required for reports or moderators?
- What will happen as a result of the assessment, particularly to those who have done badly or very well?

Once the strategy has been decided, methods appropriate to this strategy and to the aims and objectives of the course need to be devised. For example, a computer training course for adults of varied experience may choose to use a checklist of competences that learners tick off for themselves. A school mathematics tutor may decide on a series of mastery tests, and a grading examination at the end of the year. A course to develop counselling skills may use learning journals, and have periodic one-to-one tutorial sessions where issues in the journal are discussed. As always in education, the choice is made on the basis of fitness for purpose and value for effort.

Possible types of activity include the following:

- question and answer
- supply type questions
- selection type questions
- projects
- assignments
- essays
- practical tests

Tip: Devise mark schemes along with the tests and keep them safe for further use, along with a monitoring copy of the paper on which you can write suggested amendments. This enables you to improve the assessment process and allows comparison of learners from year to year. Saving and amending tests and mark schemes takes organization, but it saves many precious hours of work.

Mark schemes

Contrary to popular belief, it is unusual to give most marks for the more difficult parts of a question or paper, as this strongly biases the test in favour of the most able. It is used to apportion marks on the basis of the likely time taken by the candidate to complete the answer. Candidates should be aware of how marks are allocated. It's a good idea to mark a very good script first to check the mark scheme! If you wish to grade or discriminate, set a large number of moderately difficult questions, rather than a small number of very hard ones.

You will of course need to keep records of your assessments so always find out what has been done before. However, don't keep more records than you need. We need to be clear about why we are assessing and then to find the most appropriate technique or style to fulfil that purpose. Assessment is a creative process that can be as varied and interesting as teaching and learning. It can be fun!

Task 5.6

The task is to make and assess a greetings' card for an occasion of your small group's choice. There are a series of stages in the task:

1   Whole group: list the aspects of the card production you might want to assess. Choose some **process** and some **product** aspects, for example *'each group member played an equal part'*, *'card stands up by itself'*.
2   Work in your small groups: choose the 'special occasion' for your card. Collect your materials.
3   Meanwhile, one team of 'assessors' chooses from the flipchart five criteria by which they will assess the cards, and writes these down on a mark sheet (provided).
4   Assessors photocopy the criteria list and give one copy to each group.
5   Make the card. Assessors to circulate individually and assess in two ways:
    (a) Decide if each criterion has been met or not.
    (b) Score each criterion out of ten.
    (c) If possible, the assessors put the cards into rank order of 1st, 2nd and so on.

Case study 5.1 Sandra

Sandra, a part-time tutor who works in an FE college in Merseyside, teaches a group of 16-year-olds on the college's 'Step Up' programme* on the topic of basic customer service. She is particularly interested in how her learners actually learn but more so in how best to assess that learning.

'I'm constantly weighing up what's happening among the learners in the classroom. What I'm doing is looking for clues – or perhaps just being sensitive to clues – that will tell me how well I am teaching and how well the learners are learning. I watch what they do in their work and draw my conclusions; and, of course, I listen to what they say and ask them to explain further, so that I can understand the way their minds are working. I take soundings by observing their work, listening, questioning and even giving tests and these help me to understand what the course members have learned – and how they learn – and this enables me to help them develop further.'

*The course was renamed when NEET (not in employment, education or training) was considered derogatory.

You may have other points that you want to add but what is important is that your assessment strategy:

- focuses on the individual needs of your learners;
- as far as possible involves your learners;
- is manageable within the constraints of your work as a tutor;
- is appropriate to the learning outcomes you are facilitating.

Task 5.7

Read through the following case studies then:

- discuss them with a colleague or within your group;
- make a note of any strengths and weaknesses in the teaching, focusing on how effectively the tutor appears to be assessing the learners;
- compare notes with other members of your learning group.

Case study 5.2 Joanne

Joanne arrives at her class and begins the session. She gives brief directions about a task she has prepared and then hands out the worksheets.

One learner looks puzzled.
'I don't understand this,' another remarks.
'We've not done anything on this before', a learner at the front chips in.
'Don't know what this means', echoes a third.

Case study 5.3 Joshua

Joshua was well organized, notes ready, materials to hand and there was no doubt that he knew his subject. He was an expert in his field. He explained the causes of the rebellion, the event and the results. The learners, heads down, wrote furiously. An hour passed.

'Time up,' he said, 'I'll have to finish off next week,' and hurried to his next group.

Case study 5.4 James

It was almost the end of the session.

'Can you just stop now?' said James. 'If you haven't quite finished can you do so at home, before the next session? But before you go are there any points you don't understand? Any questions? I think you will have no difficulty with this topic if it comes up in the exam because I've just glanced at the short exercise you did earlier and you had all managed that perfectly. Nothing? Fine. I'll see you all on Thursday'.

We must aim to find the best fit between purpose, validity, reliability and manageability. We can assess by asking learners to write down, illustrate, present work graphically, speak the answers to tasks or questions or present them in writing, or orally, or in a visual or graphic form. If the assessment objective is a practical one, to check whether learners can perform a given task, then we need to observe what they do. That 'doing' may, in turn, be affected by how we present the task to them in the first place. If the purpose of our assessment is to place learners in rank order, we need to be clear about what that rank order is based on. It could be the speed by which the learner completes the task, or arriving at a correct answer or it could be the 'elegance' of the procedure that the learner goes through in reaching the correct answer in a mathematical problem, for example. If, on the other hand we are assessing to decide whether a learner has achieved a particular 'criterion', we are not concerned with measuring the learner against other learners, but only with measuring the learner's performance against the requirements of the criterion. We therefore need to know first **why** and for **what** purpose, we are doing the assessment before we decide the particular approach we need to use.

We need also to consider what we will have to do in the circumstances:

If the learner has to speak	we need to be able to listen
If the learner has to perform a task	we need to observe closely
If the learner needs to write or illustrate	we need to look at her/his efforts
If there is a tangible product	we may need to look at this away from the learner
If there is no tangible product	we may need to do the assessment at the time the task is done

We need always to be aware that, for some learners, we may be placing unnecessary barriers between their knowledge and their means of expressing and communicating that knowledge. We may end up only finding out about what the learner can write in English and not what the learner knows about the subject.

How should assessment take place?

Assessment techniques vary according to the degree to which they are either:

- formal or informal;
- norm-referenced or criterion-referenced.

Formal or informal

Formal assessment tends to be initiated by the tutor and then officially recorded either digitally or in written format for examination boards, moderation and certification. Informal assessment is often negotiated by the tutor and the learners and is unrecorded (for example classroom discussion/learners' questions).

Task 5.8

See if you can note down two examples of each type of assessment for the following stages of your programme (there is more about timing later in this section):

(*continued*)

- at the start
- during
- at the end

You could have suggested:

At the start:
Formal:

- accreditation of prior learning
- interview
- training audit
- on the job observation

Informal:

- pre-enrolment chat
- statement on application form
- self-completion questionnaire

During:
Formal:

- assignments
- observation of performance
- simulation
- tutorial/interview

Informal:

- project work
- learning journal
- peer feedback
- quizzes

At the end:
Formal:

- oral or written exam
- record of achievement
- profile of competence

Informal:

- learner-self-assessment questionnaire
- classroom discussion

When should assessment take place?

Assessment should take place at all stages of your programme. However, there are specific points in any programme when assessment may be particularly appropriate.

Pre-programme
Assessment at this and the next point is often referred to as 'diagnostic'. Carried out before a programme begins it can help course organizers to establish the need for a specific programme and maintain entry standards.

At the start of a programme
Assessment at the start of a programme helps you to design appropriate programmes, manage groupings of learners and identify likely problems. It helps your learners to gain a clearer picture of their learning needs and prepare, with your assistance, an action plan for their learning, as well as feel motivated.

At intervals within a programme
This type of assessment is often termed 'formative'. Formative assessment enables you to check whether your objectives are being met, if necessary replan your programme and check that all your learners are on an appropriate programme – and refer any that are not to alternative provision. It helps your learners to gain a sense of motivation and achievement.

At the end of a programme
This type of assessment is often termed 'summative'. Summative assessment sums up a learner's achievements at the end of a programme. It helps to determine the effectiveness of your programme and justify your programme to funders. It helps your learners to gain an award, which may in turn permit entry to employment or a further programme as well as gain a sense of achievement and is typically the basis on which an award is made.

Task 5.9 Assessment quiz

1   Norm-referencing refers to assessment in which the learner is compared to . . .

(*continued*)

2 'Behaviourist methods are not appropriate when teaching adults.' Discuss.

3 What type of assessment are the following

Assessment which occurs at the end of a course, to give learners a final grade, is. . . .

We give . . . . assessment tests during a course, to assess learners' progress.

'I watch learners while they are working. I notice any difficulties they may be having.' This type of assessment is called . . . . assessment.

4 List 6 reasons why we assess. Use the initial letter to help you decide:

D
E
G
G
S
P

Task 5.10

Answer the following questions:

1 What is the product of 5 and 8?
2 What is 5 times 8?
3 What is 8 multiplied by 5?
4 $8 \times 5 =$
5 $5 \times 8 =$
6 Eight people each give me five pounds. How much money do I now have?
7 There are 5 gallons of water in each of 8 water butts. How much water, in gallons, is there altogether?
8 What is your answer if I ask you to multiply five by eight?
9 8
$\times 5$
10 $5 \times 8 =$

- What basic knowledge is common to all these questions?
- Does each separate question make any assumptions?
- Is anything else being assessed in these questions?

Memory

An important part of any discussion about assesement methods is that of memory. It is essential to understand the capacity of learners to remember information and how we can enable them to enhance this.

The ability to retain and recall information is called memory. This can be divided into short-term and long-term memory. Memory is fundamental to learning and assessment. Consequently memory difficulties will have an impact on learning and remembering new things. Learners with short-term memory difficulties can have issues with recalling previously learned words or instructions. Sometimes referred to as 'fluctuating memory', learners can sometimes complete tasks in one session and then not in another. This will cause difficulties with assessment especially when recording the acquisition of new knowledge. Some learners with long-term memory difficulties may not learn even after several attempts and practice. However, an awareness of memory can help tutors provide appropriate learning opportunities. The short-term memory appears to retain the immediate interpretation of the events. The long-term memory appears to have a huge capacity. If information can access the long-term memory then it may be stored indefinitely.

It is the role of the tutor to help the learner to recall information during the learning session to enable the learner to store information more readily into the long-term memory if possible.

A suggested information-processing model for memory

- **Incoming information**
- **Sensory information store:** accurate and fairly complete information lasting about half a second
- **Short term memory or working memory:** limited interpretation of events held for about twenty seconds or longer if rehearsed
- **Coding process:** coding carried out at a subconscious level
- **Long term memory/conceptual structure:** effectively unlimited amount of information held indefinitely.

Memory processes

Perception and early encoding

All information acquired from the environment is received by sensory receptors which respond to a specific stimulus (for example eyes to light waves and ears to sound waves). Information remaining in the sensory memory must be recognized and processed into more concise and meaningful units by comparing it with similar information already stored in the long-term memory. After this analysis it can be passed to another limited capacity store – usually called short-term or 'working' memory.

Short-term memory (STM)

Encoding is the process by which this information can be transferred into the kind of code which the memory can accept. Encoding seems to be acoustic for verbal material (words, letters and numbers) and visual for non-verbal material. There may also be codes linked to touch, taste and smell.

Storage has limited capacity. As new items enter the STM the older ones appear to be displaced. Storage can be improved by arranging the material in meaningful units or chunks (for example phrases, familiar groups of numbers).

Retrieval involves a search of STM in which each item or chunk is examined.

Long-term memory (LTM)

Encoding is usually based on meaning using a concrete image code or an abstract semantic one. The more deeply and thoroughly the meaning is encoded the more effective will be the recall. This process of encoding is personal and shows wide variations among individuals.

Storage appears to have an almost unlimited capacity. In fact, new material is more likely to be stored effectively if there is encoded information already stored to which it can be linked. Storage is further improved by active, thorough organization on the part of the learner.

Retrieval depends on the way material in storage is organized and an appropriate cue such as a similar context. Retrieval after a period of learning improves initially, presumably because the mind needs a few minutes to sort out the new information, especially the last items. During this time all the interconnections within the new material are linked more firmly.

Forgetting things more frequently results from a failure in retrieval rather than storage. Retrieval may be helped by an organizational guide (for example initial letter of names as in the 'tip of the tongue' experience), associations (for example in function) and hierarchical organization.

Common aids for memorizing

Aids to recall

Frequency: The more you make recall active, via testing, the more likely it is that the learner will remember.

Intensity: The better the concentration, the better the recall. Ensure appropriate surroundings without distractions.

Importance: The learner remembers the most important things to them at the time. Always try to ensure that the information fits into their ongoing experience.

Feelings: The state of your mind affects the quality of learning. For example, if learners are upset about domestic issues then their ability to enhance recall will be reduced. Always try to get to know the learners and ensure support.

Association: The more you can associate and relate new material to existing knowledge, the better the recall. Try to do this with each learning session by encouraging the learners to recall their own experiences that associate with new material.

Verbal association

- Group things together, for example it costs the same to send an airmail letter to Argentina, Canada, Kenya and South Africa
- Pair things, for example knife and fork
- Link things you already know, for example Brighton is in Sussex, and Hove is near Brighton, so also in Sussex
- Make up unlikely associations, for example chalk and cheese
- Make up a story linking things together

Visual

- Group things together and visualize them
- Visualize the location, for example imagine opening the pantry door and seeing the things on the shelves to remember what food to buy
- Write a list and visualize it

Repetition

- *Written* write out a number of times, for example spelling mistakes
- *Verbal* repeat aloud a number of times, for example poetry
- *Aural* listen several times to a tape or record
- *Visual* read over and over again

Self-testing

Used in combination with repetition this is particularly helpful.

'Part' testing

If there is a lot to be learned, break it down into 'parts'. Learn each part thoroughly before going on to the next part. For older learners, it is helpful to revise the first part while learning the second part (cumulative part-learning). Test yourself on the first two parts before going on to the next part (progressive part-learning). Learning all the parts separately before testing yourself (pure part-learning) is not a good method.

Special aids for memorizing

Number rhyme

First memorize associations between numbers and rhyming systems objects, for example one-bun, two-shoe, three-tree. Then form unusual associations between the things to be remembered and the rhyming objects, for example if objects to be remembered are piano, daffodil and chocolates, one could imagine a piano piled high with buns, a shoe used as a vase for daffodils and a tree with chocolates as fruit.

Spelling associations

Where there is confusion between the spelling of similar sounding words with different meanings, for example 'stationery' and 'stationary', the correct spelling can be helped by associating stationery with envelopes.

Roman Greek

This involves having a strong mental picture of a large house or place, with a number of different rooms, passages and stairways which you can 'walk through' in your mind. You then associate each window or doorway with an idea or thing you want to remember.

Conditions for good recall

Errors	Try to avoid making mistakes.
Recency	There is a tendency to remember the last thing you read.
Frequency	The more you test yourself, the more you learn.
Intensity	The more you concentrate, the more you learn.
Importance	The more important the material is to you, the more you learn.
Affective (feelings)	Your state of mind, or how you feel, at the time of learning affects what you learn.
Association	The more you can relate the material to be learned to other things, the more you learn.

Approaches to consider

- work with learners to find memory strategies of triggers that are effective for them
- ask questions to help with retrieval and recall
- use cue cards
- topic-based lists
- post-its and prompt cards.

Technology can also be very useful in assessment of learning and can provide a very inclusive approach. Before we look at e-assessment, carry out the tasks which follow and, from the point of view of the learner, consider the effectiveness of each strategy and whether they can be incorporated into your own learning and teaching.

Task 5.11

Recognition

Underline the capital city of each country:

AFGHANISTAN	Kalida	Kasko	Kabul
AUSTRAILIA	Canberra	Cambridge	Calvert
AUSTRIA	Volga	Verga	Vienna
CANADA	Ottawa	Ostend	Overton
CHINA	Pegyash	Penglai	Peking
DENMARK	Cubango	Copenhagan	Corder
EGYPT	Cairo	Cracow	Crues
FRANCE	Paton	Percy	Paris
IRAN	Teza	Terasina	Tehran
IRELAND	Dublin	Devizes	Duren
ISRAEL	Jarana	Johannesburg	Jerusalem
ITALY	Roa	Rome	Riyadt
JAPAN	Tokyo	Tomsk	Tojo

(continued)

HOLLAND	Ambriz	Amsterdam	Amyot
NORWAY	Osorno	Osho	Oslo
SPAIN	Manabi	Madrid	Madrona
SWEDEN	Stockholm	Stockport	Salisbury

Task 5.12

Free recall

Write down the name of the capital city of each of these countries.

Afghanistan:	Japan:
Australia:	Holland:
Argentina:	Norway:
Austria:	Spain:
Canada:	Sweden:
China:	USA:
Denmark:	Ireland:
Egypt:	Iran:
France:	Israel:

Each task is appropriate to the topic 'Geography: cities' but is an example of differentiated approaches to assessment.

E-assessment

So far we have discussed classroom based assessment strategies requiring the presence of the tutor and the learners together. However, through the use of new and emerging technologies it is now possible to enhance assessment through the use of e-assessment.

E-assessment covers the use of technology/ICT for a broad range of assessments. It observes the principles of assessment as discussed earlier and can be employed to check learning in much the same way as in traditional assessment formats. However we would encourage you to consider whether adopting an e-assessment strategy actually improves the learner experience. Strategies include assessing a learner's starting point (initial assessment), checking a learner's progress midway through a course and feeding back to the learner on their progress (formative assessment) or assessing whether the learner has achieved their learning objectives by the end of a course (summative assessment).

The type of technology used to carry out the assessments could vary depending on the purpose of the assessment and what was suitable and meaningful to use with the individual learner. E-assessment approaches have the potential to make assessments more interactive and personalized for individual learners. For example, interactive quizzes utilizing voting-pads or standalone computers/laptops could be easily adapted for a range of learning styles to carry out initial, formative and summative assessments.

E-assessment is not only about using the technology to test a learner's understanding of a particular subject (for example, through multiple-choice quizzes or assessments) but it is also about using the technology to record a learner's achievement and progress. For example, a video clip showing a learner swimming a length of the pool without the use of floats can be used to demonstrate that the learner has acquired skill and confidence in swimming, which they may not have previously had.

Electronic means of initial, formative and summative assessment are very useful to the tutor and of course can make the process more engaging and fun for the learners. Think how more efficiently one might assess an audio-visual recording of an individual or a group of learners by observation of their body language or of their competence to perform an informal task. We could use this assessment to diagnose a person's strengths and weaknesses, to provide feedback on their performance and to judge whether the person has achieved the agreed learning objectives.

How can we use digital technology in assessment?

Learning/achievement can be sampled in many ways:

- A video or photograph of a role-played interview provides useful feedback to the learner as well as allowing a judgement to be made on the achievement of the learning objectives.
- A 'drag and drop' exercise can check a learner's factual recall and provide instant feedback on achievement.
- Multiple-choice questions can check a learner understands and recalls and can also provide feedback tailored to the learner's specific needs.

Some advantages and disadvantages

Setting up online assessment such as multiple-choice question tests can initially be expensive in time and software – but when it is set up there is a saving since the assessments can be used time and again. A bank of online resources can be built up, providing learners with a range of assessment opportunities to suit their level and learning needs. Open-source (free for not-for-profit educational institutions) software like 'Hot Potatoes' is available for setting up your own quizzes and there are many free resources available from NLN, Ferl and Becta. Online assessment gives the learner autonomy to make mistakes and repeat tasks in relative privacy. There are many online freeware or subscription sites which will already have assessments that have been prepared by other tutors and stored on the site according to subject areas, for example Quia.

E-portfolios

Paper portfolios are regularly used to compile a record of students' work. Often they include images and artefacts to illustrate the learner journey as well as reflective comments by the learner on the learning experience. E-portfolios can include even more information about learners' achievements and experiences. The use of an e-portfolio as a record of lifelong learning is one suggestion and already there are programmes such as *pebble pad** which are designed to promote e-learning and e-assessment. E-portfolios are also being introduced in some areas of tutor/practitioner training to record the learning journey of the trainee tutor. For example, the e-portfolio could contain the record of the learner's initial assessment, materials produced by the learner during the learning process, photographs of a finished product such as a painting, or a video of a process such as hairdressing. It could also contain feedback on the learner's work, a profile of learning styles and a detailed outline of summative achievement.

When introducing new technologies in the teaching and learning process, the intention should be to enhance the learner journey. You will engage learners in different ways to before. It is important to consider accessibility issues when introducing any new technology because it is crucial to avoid excluding learners from the learning experience.

Task 5.13

Recording learners' achievements

1   Consider a typical session with a group of learners and the type of assessment you carry out. Perhaps you use a combination of writing a report whilst observing an activity.

2 Consider ways that the learner journey could be recorded at different stages, identifying which digital technology you could use to record evidence. Be as creative and experimental as you can!

3 Consider how you could make use of the following in your teaching:

- digital cameras
- laptop and projector
- tape recorder
- Mp3 player
- Interactive whiteboard
- IPod
- wiki
- blog
- podcast
- VLE
- virtual classroom

Virtual Learning Environments (VLEs)

Below are some of the main VLEs and conferencing packages that you may come across. We are not promoting or excluding any particular products but we have listed those which, along with our colleagues, we use or have used in the past. Your organization may have developed its own platform or even written their own VLEs.

Producers of commercial VLEs

- Blackboard® (http://www.blackboard.com)
- Fronter (http://fronter.info/uk)
- WebCT (http://www.webct.com).

Free or open-source VLEs

There are various free VLEs available, often where the development has been funded by government agencies. Open-source software is that where the source code is available for download, and can be changed freely. An example is Moodle (http://moodle.org).

Task 5.14

1   Identify which VLE is used or preferred by your organization. This will mean scrutinizing its functions and capacities beyond that of a mere repository of resources. Think how the learners' experiences are enhanced and focus on how assessment and feedback might be also made more accessible.
2   Identify five ways you could use your VLE to enhance your sessions.

Creating resources using a range of software applications

It is extremely useful to know that there is a wide range of software and freeware available to help practitioners create new and innovative resources. Again we need to emphasize that the resources should enhance the learner experience rather than being used for the sake of it, so once you have read through the following list of resources think about how you can use the lesser known ones to enhance your teaching.

Microsoft Office

This suite of products offers a range of opportunities for tutors. Microsoft Word can be used to create a variety of learning resources including interactive elements such as drag and drop or multiple-choice activities. Microsoft PowerPoint can be used to create and deliver interactive learning resources. Each slide may contain text, graphics, animation, internal and external hyperlinks, and audio and video clips. Microsoft® Excel® drop down boxes allow tutors to create simple multiple-choice exercises that can provide instant feedback. Microsoft® Photo Story allows you to create slideshows showing images with the added advantage of text, recorded narration to each slide and inserted music.

Hot Potatoes™

The Hot Potatoes™ software suite is a set of six authoring tools enabling the creation of interactive activities in a variety of styles that can run smoothly in any web browser. There are also instructions for incorporating images and sounds into Hot Potatoes™ activities.

Audacity

Audacity is free, open-source software for recording and editing sounds. It is an easy tool to use to produce narrations to accompany a learning resource or to create realistic language tasks.

> ## Task 5.15
>
> Review a particular assessment strategy you have used, preferably a learner-centred approach, and consider how the above software could be useful to enhance the experience for learners. Record the advantages and disadvantages of using the new resources considering the principles of assessment for example validity, reliability and manageability.

Chapter summary

Assessment theory and methodology is diverse and open to interpretation as to its purpose, timeliness and impact on learning. What is clear however is that a firm grasp of the key principles of assessment including e-assessment, a variety of method and application and a clear mapping of strategy to learning outcomes are the ingredients to successful learning. To experiment and to be creative are the drivers behind effective assessment which we are certain will be welcomed and embraced by all learners.

Further reading

Jarvis, P. (2006) *The Theory and Practice of Teaching*, 2nd edn. London: RoutledgeFalmer.

Maier, P. and Barnet, L. (1998) *Using Technology in Teaching and Learning*. London: Kogan Page.

6 Behaviour for learning

What is this chapter about?

This chapter looks at behaviour for learning in the 14–19 sector. It considers how to plan for good behaviour and how to manage bad behaviour. It also focuses on the differences we might come across when teaching the different ages and contexts that exist within the sector.

We begin by explaining behaviour for learning and how the three key elements – planning, engaging learners and rewarding success – can help us to experience pain-free teaching with minimum disruption and poor behaviour. Next we focus on how to manage bad behaviour when it occurs in your classroom and how to deal consistently and fairly with any disruption. We consider what causes students to misbehave, including some of the syndromes and conditions and the social factors that affect learners. Throughout, the chapter aims to give practical hints and tips on how to plan for and manage behaviour in the classroom.

Task 6.1 Preliminary reading

Vizard, D. (2007) *How to Manage Behaviour in Further Education.* London: Paul Chapman.
Wallace, S. (2007) *Managing Behaviour in the Lifelong learning Sector.* Exeter: Learning Matters.

Behaviour for learning

Tutors are frequently concerned with how to manage the behaviour of younger learners who are perhaps still at school and attend college for vocational subjects as part of the 14–19 agenda as well as those young people who have chosen to study vocational subjects at college post 16. Many feel that young people are not necessarily choosing programmes at 14 because they have a genuine interest in that vocational area; rather there is often nothing else to choose or they are strongly 'advised' to take that option because it is a way of getting them out of school or away from doing standard GCSEs. Some schools use vocational options as a way of managing the more disruptive students so they can focus on those who will achieve 5 A*–C grades at GCSE.

Once young people leave school at 16 they then have the option to choose to continue in education and to take any of a wide range of vocational or academic qualifications. However with the advent of the educational maintenance allowance (EMA), and the need for many parents to continue to claim benefits for children who are still in education, then this 'choice' becomes more of a compulsion. There are many tutors/practitioners who state how demotivating it is for them when their learners seem to be interested only in collecting their EMA rather than in the opportunity to learn or gain a qualification. The education maintenance allowance was launched in 2004 and is a scheme which pays young people from low-income families to stay on in education after the age of 16. Roughly 545,000 young people have signed up to receive the allowance since it started, according to figures supplied by the Learning and Skills Council. It is currently under review in the programme of government spending cuts.

Other concerns include teaching learners whose first language is not English or those who are disenchanted, aggressive, indifferent, apathetic, need social care and special attention, or are demanding and ambitious and need to be stretched.

We can see then that the 14–19 education and training sector is very diverse and is rapidly changing. There are more and more young people in education who are demotivated or disengaged and this must be reflected in how we manage the behaviour of learners. This means taking into account changes in teaching and learning that will be needed to engage 14–19-year-old learners and to consider the effect these may have on the behaviour we observe in the classroom and the strategies we employ to ensure learning is taking place.

'Behaviour for learning' as opposed to 'managing behaviour' implies a shift in attitude from tutors/practitioners and puts the emphasis on their responsibility to plan for good behaviour instead of expecting the worst. 'Behaviour for learning' is not a traditional theory but more of a movement to change the emphasis from managing bad behaviour to planning for good behaviour. This, for some tutors at least, will be a new way of thinking. It implies a key role for tutors in improving learners' attitudes and in taking responsibility for their role in incidents of unsatisfactory conduct that occur in their classrooms. There is an emphasis on the crucial link between the way in which young people learn and their social knowledge and behaviour. The focus is upon establishing positive relationships, setting clear ground rules for behaviour, being consistent in our dealings with learners and praising and rewarding success.

Young people coming into 14–19 education have often had a negative experience in school and we have a valuable role to play in providing an opportunity for learners to re-engage with learning. As a result of research and personal experience we believe that behaviour for learning can be split into three components:

- planning
- engaging learners
- rewarding success.

Planning

Detailed planning enables the tutor to be proactive rather than reactive in establishing a suitable environment for learning. 'If the tutor does not give the impression of competence, knowledge and the ability to control and direct learning, then the learners will switch off very quickly and will show their frustration by behaving badly' (Keeley-Browne 2007).

Planning sessions to avoid situations that might trigger bad behaviour and thinking about possible triggers in advance is likely to reduce the opportunities for behaviour to deteriorate. But it is also about planning for and expecting good behaviour. If we set high standards in our expectations of students then they are more likely to live up to those standards.

Case study 6.1

As a Travel and Tourism lecturer I have taken students on many residential visits to several countries over the years. In the early days we used to search out the most basic youth hostels to stay in so that the students did not cause any problems or do any damage. What we found was that although it was true that they did not upset 'real' holidaymakers with their behaviour, the standard of their behaviour fell to the standard of the accommodation and the other parties staying there.

One year we were going to Prague and could only find accommodation in a very nice hotel. I was extremely concerned about the students' ability to behave appropriately in such good accommodation, but was amazed to find out that they respected the environment and the trust we had shown in them by taking them somewhere nice and behaved in a much more responsible and mature way. They lived up to our expectations because they were pleased that we valued them enough to take them somewhere nice. We found out that the higher the standard of accommodation the better they behaved and the easier it was for the staff.

Task 6.2

Think about any other situations in which this technique might work. Do you use it with your students?

Ground rules

In order to behave well, learners need to be very clear what the ground rules are and what the consequences of breaking the rules will be. Lecturers who involve learners in drawing up ground rules and in signing up to those rules, and who consistently apply those consequences, should experience less disruption and bad behaviour. Learners will be aware of the rules, feel an ownership of them and will see that they are being implemented fairly. Your organization will have a code of conduct or similar set of rules for students to follow. However, it is good practice to set your own rules for your own classroom.

For example, you may agree to allow students to listen to their iPods when they are working alone on tasks, but to put them away when working in groups or listening to you. You may agree to them talking while they are working as long as they are on task, or to enjoy five minute chat breaks when key tasks have been completed. Think carefully about the rules you want and make sure you allow students some room to negotiate. It goes without saying that there is no negotiation about things such as treating others with respect, not swearing and complying with health and safety regulations, but there may be room for negotiations about food and drink, clothing and talking.

You may find that each group you teach will set slightly different ground rules, but as long as they sign up to and follow them, this is good. It does no harm to restate those rules at the beginning of sessions particularly for the first few weeks, so that no one 'gets into trouble' for forgetting the rules. It is also a good idea to get students either to make a poster or print out a list of the rules and individually sign them and display them on the classroom walls. This allows you to use this as a visual prompt to remind students of what they have agreed to.

Many authors (Vizard 2007; Petty 2010) support the view that setting clear ground rules *with* students and not *for* students will raise expectations of good behaviour and will allow them to buy into the process and feel valued and secure in the classroom. In some cases the learners become self-policing, quickly identifying when others in the group are breaking a rule and challenging them. This allows you to manage the learning environment in a less controlling way.

Task 6.3

Identify one of your teaching groups and negotiate a set of ground rules with them. Give them the responsibility to sign and display them in the classroom. Refer to them constantly and see if this helps manage behaviour.

Planning sessions

The quality of session planning will have a direct effect on behaviour in the classroom. If you are disorganized and unprepared then there will be more unstructured time in which students can become distracted and disengaged. If you keep them busy and on task every second of the session then they have less opportunity to become bored and so get into trouble. The vast majority of young people who are disruptive in class cite boredom as the major cause. It is our responsibility as tutors to make our sessions as interesting as possible. There is always going to be the case where whatever we do the student is going to be 'bored' and there is a growing culture among some young people to affect 'boredom' in all situations, which can be infuriating.

For example, a colleague of ours was bemoaning the fact that he had spent six hours preparing a game for his class to check their learning only for them to say it was boring and for it not to work. On reflection over coffee we came to realize that the game was so complicated that it was difficult for the students to follow and they quickly lost attention. They were actually disengaged rather than bored but unable to articulate how they were feeling. We need to make sure that learning is taking place in an engaging way that is appropriate to the learners and the curriculum. Students will quickly see through time-wasting activities and games but can often be very focused on their assignments or exams. If they feel that the planned activity is not helping them to pass those assignments or exams then they will lose focus and in some cases behave badly.

Although our teaching should command interest, our purpose is to educate and not just entertain. Each session we plan should have a clear set of objectives that is shared with the learners and which they can understand and see a purpose to. At the end of the session we should re-visit those objectives and clearly demonstrate how they have been achieved. Students will then feel that their time has not been wasted and they are making progress towards their overall learning goal. Remember, it is very hard to be 'naughty' when you are interested in the session and learning is taking place.

Group work

Group work is already a common feature of many classrooms. Whether in the form of pairs or larger groupings, it can be a highly effective way of working and learning, taking advantage of the combined strengths of the different members of a team. However, if managed ineffectively, little learning may take place. Tutors need to be particularly aware of the make-up of groups, for example of the underlying tensions and issues in a class, and should get students used to working with a variety of others.

Subtly reflecting this in the planning ensures that learning can take place and signals to the learners that the teacher is aware of and listening to their concerns. You always need to have a clear rationale for choosing groups and this should be explicit in your planning documentation so that an observer is clear as to your motives.

> ## Case study 6.2: Jackson, example of a rationale for a group work activity
>
> My teaching and learning activities for this session have been designed to build up the existing knowledge and practical experience that trainees have from their placements and previous educational experiences. A variety of activities has been planned to keep the attention of the trainees, as even though they are adult learners they can have a short attention span. I have not limited the teaching and learning activities to the learning styles of this cohort as the Coffield Report suggests that learners benefit from being challenged by different learning activities. However, I will bear in mind their learning styles and support appropriately. I have designed learning activities
>
> *(continued)*

which are accessible to all the learners, with support, and that will not exclude any learner (Wallace 2005). I want to promote inclusiveness during the session which I will achieve by explaining any unclear words, giving specific instructions, providing handouts on coloured paper and supporting learners as required. In this session trainees will be split into four groups based on random selection. They will be given a coloured spot on arrival and will have to sit on that table. I have chosen to split them in this manner as it encourages them to work with people other than their immediate friendship groups and to get to know other learners in the group.

The tutor should be aware that establishing groups requires some thought and planning to avoid problems which are sometimes caused by issues such as gender and friendship. (For further ideas on this see Clarke 2005.) Groups normally consist of approximately six learners, depending on attendance, and this is appropriate because the nature of the tasks in this session has a focus on discussion and larger groups will facilitate this. Discussions are effective learning strategies that allow students to express, share and develop ideas. For the maximum benefit it may be necessary for students to make some notes as a record of the discussion and the key points that emerge. Providing explicit instructions to students helps them to see what is expected of them. It can help them to plan their work and prepare effectively for sessions. It is particularly helpful for those students who find it difficult to organize themselves. This is often the case for students with conditions such as dyslexia or those with mental health difficulties (Holloway 2004). It is part of the process of providing the 'big picture', one of the key stages in what is sometimes called the Accelerated Learning Cycle (Smith 1996). In this example the rationale for the two learning activities are:

'A professional tutor activity': This activity is designed to promote group work and to draw on the experiences of the trainees in their placements. The groups are asked to identify what they believe a professional tutor is and is not. This is then shared with the whole group and will form the basis of a whole class discussion. Cooperation between and within groups of learners and tutors/practitioners is essential for effective learning. Cooperation depends on trust and trust promotes cooperation. An agreed set of rules for group work and discussion helps to promote trust and cooperation. It also makes classroom management easier (Clarke 2005).

'Pledge activity': This is used to reinforce the proposed session objectives and to check learning. Each group decides on their own definition of

professionalism as it applies to them, and then produces a pledge signed by them all to demonstrate their commitment to that pledge.

Planning and organizing groups for group work activities beforehand and having this already on the desks or on the board makes it clear to learners that it is non-negotiable. They also have time to adjust to the planned activity. Try to avoid too much change during a session. Put students into groups as they come into the class and then stick with those throughout the session unless there is a clear need to change things around. If you want it to appear that the group choices are random then use jigsaw pieces, sticky dots or Post-it® notes as they enter the room. You can still control who you put in which group but it can be less contentious if you make it appear random and not that you are splitting up friendship groups.

Task 6.4

Prepare a rationale for a group work activity that you use in your teaching. Does this help you to focus your planning?

Being a reflective practitioner

> Reflection is an important human activity in which people recapture their experience, think about it, mull it over and evaluate it. It is working with experience that is important in learning.
>
> (Boud 1985: 124)

Tutors need to reflect on their experiences in the classroom and adapt their strategies accordingly:

> By reflecting critically, instead of continuing with our feelings of self doubt, we can become positive in our search for new understandings of our practice and more ways to deal with the challenges that confront us continually. We take control over our professional practice, acknowledging that we cannot transform everything, but aware that we can identify the spheres in which we can. It is a truly emancipatory process.
>
> (Hillier 2005: 20)

In reflecting on experiences of bad behaviour in the classroom it is important to acknowledge the extent of the tutor's own responsibilities and the extent to which their actions have influenced the behaviour of the learners. By acknowledging their own role in the incident they can devise strategies for responding differently in the future. Being perceptive to the dynamics of the class and the internal relationships that exist will help to avoid situations where disruptive conduct can become an issue. Tutors need to develop emotional intelligence and be able to empathize with and understand the triggers that cause bad behaviour.

Daniel Goleman defines emotional intelligence as our ability to be able to motivate ourselves, persist in the face of frustrations, control impulses, regulate our moods and keep distress from swamping our ability to think, to empathize with others and to hope (Goleman 1996). The fact that we have the ability to control these emotions does not mean that we always do and it takes time and practice to become 'emotionally intelligent' and to use those skills in understanding our learners. Being able to read body language is another essential tool that allows the lecturer to anticipate and respond quickly to tensions and issues as they arise in the classroom.

Task 6.5

Think about your most 'challenging' group of learners and reflect on strategies that have worked and those that have not worked. Are there any key themes that emerge?

Engaging learners

Young people often experience a barrier to learning when something else occupies their minds, preventing them from focusing the necessary attention on what is to be learnt. There are so many different things that can cause young people to get distracted or disengaged from learning and it is the lecturer's job to manage the learning experience. Young people are particularly vulnerable to peer pressure and to emotional reactions to external situations. We can often see the consequences of this in the classroom when their emotional distress manifests itself in bad or disruptive behaviour. Often it is enough to be aware of these influences and empathize with the young person, removing them from the situation and talking calmly though the causes of the emotional reaction. According to Wallace (2007) tutors/practitioners can't manage any situation unless they take accurate notice of what is happening with their learners and the dynamics in the classroom.

As we have seen, sessions need to be well structured and planned to engage learners in the learning. Activities should be interesting, varied and valuable and the objectives for each activity should be shared with the learners. Learners are less likely to misbehave if they are engaged and working hard. Behaviour for learning encourages lecturers to take time and effort in the planning of interesting sessions that are enjoyable and that ensure learning is taking place. Tutors are also responsible for ensuring equality and fairness in the classroom: 'All students must feel that they are positively and equally valued and accepted, and that their efforts to learn are recognized, and judged without bias' (Petty 2004: 81).

The second key factor in behaviour for learning is to make sure students are always engaged in their learning and that work is neither too easy or too difficult. Differentiation is essential to ensure that the needs of all learners are planned for and work is suitable for all learners: ' "Differentiation" is adopting strategies that ensure success in learning for all, by accommodating individual differences of any kind' (Petty 2004: 541).

Learners in this sector are very diverse. Therefore using a wide range of resources will engage and motivate the learners by matching, wherever possible, the range of their needs. There are many differences between learners that affect their learning. Differentiation is about coping with these differences and using them to promote learning. Differentiated learning takes into account that learners may differ in terms of their motivation, prior experience and knowledge, learning support needs, cultural expectations, literacy, language, numeracy and ICT levels, and their learning preferences.

It is important to develop resources that cover more than one level of difficulty. Use different media or give choices of how to complete tasks and provide learning support where necessary (Gravells and Simpson 2008). Differentiation enables all learners to participate in learning and reduces the chance of bad behaviour occurring. This personalization of learning is very important and ensures that learners feel valued and supported. Working in this sector requires a commitment from tutors to adopt this ethos, where every learner matters and every learner's learning needs should be accommodated (Keeley-Browne 2007).

When planning and delivering sessions, it is an important goal to mix the range of activities. Using a range of group work and individual work, active and quiet learning, 'de-fizz' activities and brain gym will ensure that learners are engaged throughout the session. Using de-fizz activities after a fun and lively activity will allow students to calm down and to think about the activity they have just done. This can be as simple as completing an evaluation sheet at the end of the group task. This will allow them to work alone and will bring the level of 'fizz' down before you introduce more activity. Similarly if you have been doing a quiet individual activity for a period of time, it is a good idea to introduce a quick 'brain gym' activity to re-engage learners and liven them up. Some of our favourite books for creative activities are listed in Box 6.1.

Box 6.1

50 Templates for Teaching and Learning by Nigel Fisher: This book contains a CD-Rom with 50 templates you can adapt and use in the classroom. I particularly like the brain drops and the snowballing activities. A key strength of this text is that it also includes a rationale for each activity that is linked to theory.

The Creative Teaching and Learning Toolkit by Brin Best and Will Thomas: This book contains a CD-Rom with activities that supplement those outlined in the book. It clearly explains how to use each activity and what you need to prepare.

A Toolkit for Creative Teaching in Post Compulsory Education by Linda Eastwood et al.: This book contains 50 activities that you can use in the classroom. It also includes a useful section about the danger points of each activity.

We Can Work it Out by the Association of Mathematics Teachers: This book contains activities you can photocopy to use as brain gym activities in any classroom or specifically in numeracy sessions.

Task 6.6

Take one handout that you use in your teaching and 'differentiate' it to offer structured tasks to meet the needs of the full range of ability levels. How easy or difficult was this?

Rewarding success

One of the most useful ways of engaging students is to reward good behaviour and encourage and reward achievement. Each learner must be respected and valued for who and what she is and a relationship of trust must be built between the lecturer and the learner. This is expressed by Rogers (1983) as 'unconditional positive regard'. The lecturer must demonstrate unconditional positive regard for each learner to ensure the learner feels safe and valued.

If the lecturer is rewarding the learner with trust and respect and by using praise to reinforce good behaviour then the learner is unlikely to want to break that trust by behaving badly (Wallace 2007). Many learners in FE have very low self-esteem so by giving out nuggets of praise when it is warranted we can enhance their feelings of self-worth and competence by acknowledging their qualities and strengths (Vizard 2007). The point about praise being warranted is often overlooked. Even very young children will learn to see through commendation which they know they have not earned.

The aim of the lecturer is to create a safe learning environment that promotes tolerance, respect and cooperation between learners and lecturers. By using behaviour-for-learning strategies the classroom will be an environment in which learners are able to participate, voice their opinions, ask questions and be actively involved in how they will learn. By demonstrating emotional intelligence and fostering 'unconditional positive regard' for all learners, lecturers will encourage students to feel valued as individuals who will then be more likely to be engaged and behave in a positive way.

One of the ways we teach trainee tutors is to model good practice with our own teaching. In other words we teach them as they should teach their young learners. To demonstrate how to manage behaviour I use a range of techniques including the use of stickers and prizes. The following example shows how powerful this can be. I use some little glass stars that I got from Dave Vizard's website in class to demonstrate how to reward success. One of my trainee tutors was a mature man who was new to teaching and a little reluctant to engage with some of my techniques. At the end of one session where he had contributed well I gave him a little blue star and quietly said to him 'Thank you for joining in today – you are a star.' Two years later I met him at his graduation event and he came up to me and holding out the little blue star he said 'I carry this with me everywhere. Believe it or not that was the first time anyone had ever praised me in class. I can see now how valuable praise is as a tool. Thank you.' Sometimes it is the simplest things that mean the most to people.

Looking after students: our duty of care

Case study 6.3: Andrew

Andrew teaches combined NVQ level 1 and GCSE food technology to a group of 14 Year 10 learners from a local high school. This is the second

(*continued*)

year he has taught a group of Year 10 students from this school. Each year manages to throw up new challenges due to the wide range of individual learning needs. This year's cohort includes students recognized as gifted and talented, as well as five students with special educational needs. All students initially struggle with studying in an adult learning environment, mainly due to the unique learning facilities of the course. Students are taught within a kitchen more commonly associated with the preparation and cooking of restaurant grade dishes. So for the students the change in environment is immense.

As with all learners the key focus of the initial weeks revolves around health and safety and the college contract of what is expected from learners and what they can come to expect from the college. However, the fact that students have been informed about their obligations to their studies doesn't guarantee that they will oblige. Learning strategies for these students have to take into account that the class is taught for three hours and occasionally in extreme temperatures (28 degrees plus). Resources have to be planned meticulously to ensure that all learners achieve, and behaviour management of all learners is effective.

This case study is a timely reminder of the lecturer's duty of care to the student. Because the learner in this instance will be using industrial cookers, ovens, steamers and professional knives, they have to be aware of the consequences of their actions. Similar risks arise in other subject areas too. Poor behaviour management can only exacerbate such risks and as a tutor you will constantly need to ask yourself the following: Are the students on task? Are they working in a safe manner? Are they observing safe working practices? Are there any possible risks to themselves and their fellow students?

One approach to handling this responsibility is to frequently stop, reflect and ask yourself the following question: 'If I was a parent of one these children, would I consider what I am doing or contemplating doing to be reasonable and prudent in all circumstances?' The answer should take into account:

1   the nature of the task;
2   any hazards that could be reasonably anticipated;
3   the steps necessary to avoid or mitigate the risks flowing from the hazards;
4   the age, ability, aptitude and special educational needs of the pupils;

5   the environment in which the task is to take place;
6   any LA or school procedures that have to be followed.

As we discussed earlier, learning processes for school students are completely different to those for 16-plus (androgogy versus pedagogy). Teaching methods have to be suitable for younger learners to ensure that they are sufficiently challenged and tasks are chunked; this keeps younger learners focused on the task in hand and also manages time limits and provides learners with short term boundaries.

Due to the lack of e-learning opportunities within the practical kitchen, students are encouraged to touch, taste, create, identify key flavours and textures, visualize their dishes and experiment with ingredient substitution to evaluate different learning outcomes. Learners benefit from this practical environment, and flourish due to its sensory nature; it appeals to the younger learner due to their naturally inquisitive thought processes: how does this happen, work, fit together, affect the outcome and so on? Ideally information taught from the tutor should be approximately 20 per cent, mostly demonstrated. 80 per cent should involve the students trying to repeat the task, while identifying the key issues, points, terminology, and so on. Thus you are developing a deep learning process through discussing and reflecting on the overall results of what has been prepared.

For 16-plus learners, there is more conviction to control their own depth of achievement. Completion of tasks is about developing, stretching and refining new found skills; developing a greater sense of autonomy, reflection and personal development. Chunking of tasks also benefits these learners but greater emphasis is placed upon tailoring material through individual learning styles questionnaires, since individual information about school students is not disseminated through to us from school.

Managing 'bad' behaviour

As with most situations in teaching there is no easy solution to behaviour issues. The important thing is for tutors to plan for positive behaviour, avoid triggers for bad behaviour and to recognize and avoid the wrong solutions. These wrong solutions can undermine the learner's confidence or motivation, are likely to make matters worse or will put the tutor in an impossible predicament. Choosing the course of action to take should be based on careful reflection and consideration of our professional values and not simply a reactive response.

Task 6.7 Behaviour scenarios

Discuss how you would feel and how you would react in the following situations and what action you would take.

1   Rachel and Catherine are painting their nails during your class.
2   Shirley, Christine and Helen are lovely but need careful handling. If you stay friends, they work – but if you get on the wrong side of them... They keep whispering to one another while the other members of the class are reporting back on their projects. It's putting the speakers off and it's maddening because, when the three of them had their say all the others listened to them. You've asked them to be quiet several times now. They say 'Sorry' and go quiet for a couple of minutes. Then they start talking again.
3   Amir has his IPod plugged into his ears. You're trying to talk to him. You have already asked him to take it off once.
4   Loretta works if she has your attention, but becomes very stroppy and attention seeking the minute you are helping somebody else or talking to the group as a whole. It's because she finds reading so difficult...
5   You are trying to show Martin how to complete the task. You are going through it step by step. He thinks he can do it without this help. You are not so sure. He suddenly turns on you and says you are treating him as though he's stupid and that your sessions are really boring anyway.
6   Philip and David are mercilessly making fun of one of the weaker boys in the group, who is trying his best. The rest of the group is becoming very abusive.
7   Arthur and Sandra are having a shouting match in the middle of the class. He has taken the chisel she was about to use. Things are getting increasingly heated and the language is certainly deteriorating. The others are loving it.
8   You have invited in an outside speaker. Things go well at first, but he's been talking for half an hour now and the kids are getting extremely restless. An undercurrent of chatter is growing...
9   Wayne tells you to .... off and then starts doing his best to distract his mates who were previously working – noisily, but quite effectively.
10 Everyone appears to be working, when Kevin suddenly starts playing music on his phone and announces 'This session is a waste of time... How much longer do we have to do this stupid work?'

A constructive approach to managing 'bad' or 'poor' behaviour consists of five key elements as follows:

1 identifying the triggers
2 early intervention
3 consistency
4 use of language (including body language)
5 consequences.

If we take a look at each one of these in turn we can identify ways of avoiding or at least managing disruptive behaviour.

Identifying the triggers

When talking about young people's behaviour I often use the analogy of a bottle of coke. If you take a bottle of coke and shake it up and then try and take the lid off, it will explode all over the place. The same is true of young people. If they get shaken up (upset, confused, embarrassed or angry) and then you confront them (take the lid off the situation) they will often explode. This may manifest itself in anger, confrontation, tears or violent behaviour. If we learn to identify the triggers (when they are getting shaken up) we can choose not to confront them and allow them time to settle down before we quietly talk through the situation.

Remember we are the adults in the situation and are quite capable of being objective and dispassionate about what is happening. Young people find it very difficult to control their emotions and will often behave badly and then when they have calmed down be able to see clearly what they did wrong.

When asked, young people can often identify their own triggers including the following reasons:

- I felt silly.
- People were laughing at me.
- I was embarrassed.
- I couldn't do the work.
- You were picking on me.
- It wasn't my fault.
- It wasn't fair.

What we need to do is be able to avoid the triggers or at least identify them as they occur and then deal with them quickly and calmly. Allow the young person a few minutes to calm down; do not shout or confront them straightaway as they will still be in the stage where they cannot manage their feelings and it will escalate very quickly into a no-win situation.

When the young person has had time to calm down, speak quietly to them and ask them to stay behind for a couple of minutes at the end of the session for a chat.

There is absolutely no value in trying to tell students off in front of their peers as they will be embarrassed and may become difficult. By having a quiet chat at the end of the session and really listening to the student, giving them time to reflect on their own behaviour and the opportunity to tell you why it occurred, you will hopefully develop an understanding of their triggers and develop a more positive relationship with them.

Task 6.8

Looking back at Task 5.7, for each situation identify what triggers it. Could it have been avoided?

Early intervention

Intervening early in situations that are likely to become triggers is an absolutely key skill for you to develop. We tend to get bogged down in trying to deliver our teaching and become preoccupied with the Power-Point, etc. rather than observing the behaviour that is occurring in the classroom.

Classrooms are like pressure cookers. We put a random mix of young people into a room and expect them all to get on with each other. Realistically this is not always going to happen, and we need to have eyes in the back of our heads and to take note of any changes in the 'vibe' or 'temperature' of the room. By being able to spot any occurrences early we can subtly take action by adapting our teaching to deal quietly with these situations. By introducing a new activity at just the right moment we can take the heat out of a potential situation and move students around without them knowing why we have done it. By being emotionally intelligent and understanding body language we can pre-empt situations from escalating into major situations. The key to this is learning your learners. Get to know them and their moods and behaviours. This will allow you to identify any changes that are occurring and deal with them early.

Consistency

Being consistent is one of our most important tools but also one of the most difficult to master. We can all remember instances from our own education where we have been treated unfairly. Been told off for talking when others are talking, or being criticized for our contributions when others are contributing less. We feel very keenly any inequality in fairness or consistency in our treatment, whether it is actual or perceived. Dave Vizard talks about consistency modelling in his book *How to Manage Behaviour in Further Education* (2007) emphasizing how we must model and clearly articulate a consistent message on behaviour to our students.

If we have a rule of no talking, then we *must* challenge *all* instances where students are talking and not just the instance which finally makes us snap. This is why we have to think very carefully about the ground rules for our classrooms as discussed earlier as we don't want to set ourselves up to fail. We need manageable rules that we can enforce easily and still have a positive learning environment. Learning should not all be about rules and being told off but should also be fun and exciting.

So think carefully about your rules and what you are prepared to enforce. For example you could have a no-talking-when-I-am-talking rule rather than a no-talking rule. This way if you are relaxed about them chatting while they are working on tasks they will be more likely to abide by the rule and not talk when you are talking. In any case it is easier to be consistent in enforcing this rule.

Many young people (especially girls) expect to be treated fairly and react very badly at perceived unfairness. If you are aware you have been unfair or are going to be unfair then be quick to apologize and give a reason for the unfair situation. For example, if you have previously allowed them to use an iPod during individual work but today need them not to, then say clearly 'I am aware that it is unfair but today I really need you to concentrate on this task so no one will be allowed to use their iPods.' It is important that we respect students' desires and needs and are humble enough to admit when we get it wrong.

Use of language

Jason Bangbala speaks frequently and eloquently about behaviour at conferences and refers often to the use of language. A key mantra of his is 'Don't say please, say thank you.' What he means is that by saying 'Please will you be quiet' we are giving students the choice about following our request. It is phrased as an option. However, if we say 'Thank you for being quiet' we are phrasing it as something that is a given. We are accepting that they are going to be quiet. 'Thank you for sitting on your chair properly' is much better than saying 'Please sit on your chair properly.' Although saying please is polite, it makes us seem less in control, whereas a firm thank you suggests control and strength.

Also critically important are our tone of voice and our air of confidence. Students can sense weakness from miles away and will be far more likely to misbehave if you show any fear, weakness or lack of confidence. Here are our top ten ways to help you show such confidence:

1   Always give instructions with confidence and certainty, even if you are unsure – you can always deal with any errors later.
2   Speak clearly, slowly and project your voice.
3   Avoid phrases like 'please can you...', 'if you would...', 'could you...' etc.
4   Use phrases like 'thank you for...', 'well done for...', 'I am pleased that you have...'.
5   Use positive body language.
6   Dress smartly.
7   Know your subject well.
8   Manage your classroom.
9   Patrol your space.
10   Be prepared for anything.

Body language

Body language is one of our most subtle, yet important, modes of communication. Understanding body language, or non-verbal communication, enables us to positively develop our communication styles, and improve relationships with people around us. In short, the ability to read and understand body language can help us to achieve success in so many areas of life, particularly in education.

Applying the right kind of body language can substantially improve the way we communicate in the classroom, reinforcing the spoken word. It helps to drive any situation in the direction that you want it to go, giving you control and confidence. Likewise, giving off the right body language signals can also help you to achieve positive relationships with students, as well as helping to diffuse difficult or volatile situations. Body language is a large part of what we 'say' as humans: it is estimated that we can produce up to 700,000 signs, including 250,000 different facial expressions and 5,000 different hand gestures in a day. There are many ways our body language can be interpreted and it is important as tutors/practitioners to be aware of the impact of this on our students.

Here are our top tips for body language:

1   Eye contact
  • Using eye contact can engage attention, display our interest and also indicate intent.
  • When meeting and greeting use eye contact.

- At the start of the session scan the whole group, engage in longer eye contact with the 'influencers' in the group.
- Staring into the distance or at the ground gives off passive/frightened messages.
- The 'eye dip' is a submissive gesture.
- Avoid the 'eye shuttle' – this is a startled response.
- If a student is misbehaving get into the student's line of sight and establish eye contact with a stare.

2 Positioning
- Give your instruction and then move away to allow them time to conform.
- When speaking to the class stand in a position where you can scan the whole group.
- It is important psychologically for you to be able to see the whole group.

3 Patrolling
- It is essential that you patrol your territory frequently.
- Visit all areas of the room.
- Patrol the perimeter of the room – keeping the maximum number of students within your line of sight.
- Stand at the back of the room for a period of time – it puts students at a psychological disadvantage.
- If problems are developing move towards the disruptive student while still talking to the class and just rest your hand on their desk.

4 Proximity
- Standing behind a student who is not working, slightly within their personal space but without saying anything, can be powerful.
- Each person has their own personal space; if anyone goes inside this space we feel threatened. When angry more personal space is likely to be needed, so it is important when dealing with students that we do not appear to be invading their personal space, which might provoke confrontation.

5 Level
- Standing over a student while they are working can be very intimidating.
- Sitting at the same level or crouching at a slightly lower level can lead to more effective communication and reduce the likelihood of increasing conflict.

6 Posture
- Posture is very important, so try and stand upright with a straight back during formal parts of the session.

- Standing with your feet slightly apart is a confident posture.
- Stand with an open posture. Avoid closed body language, such as folded arms.

7   Bodily orientation
- The angle and direction in which your body points is said to indicate your feelings.
- If you point away from a person it creates a negative perception.
- Avoid standing face to face as this can inflame conflict.
- It is best to stand at right angles to the person in conflict situations.

8   Facial expressions
- 'Our faces are the mirrors to our minds' (Roffey 2004).
- Frowning and the raising of the eyebrows indicate disapproval.
- Increased blinking is a sign of anxiety.
- A narrowing of the eyes is a signal of control or dominance.
- Lowering of the eyebrows gives the impression of dominance.
- If the mouth is set into a resolute position without smiling this can be very controlling.
- Symmetrical smiles are seen as sincere.
- Asymmetrical smiles are seen as insincere.
- The 'jaw thrust' is a gesture of defiance or control and a sign of dominance.

9   Types of body language
- Brisk erect walk = Confidence
- Clearing throat = Sign of doubt
- Arms crossed on chest = Defensiveness
- Locked ankles = Apprehension
- Biting nails = Insecurity, nervousness
- Gaze off = Dislike or disagreement
- Looking down, face turned away = Disbelief
- Rubbing the eye = Doubt, disbelief
- Patting/fondling hair = Lack of self confidence
- Pulling or tugging at ear = Indecision
- Standing with hands on hips = Readiness, aggression
- Hands clasped behind back = Anger, frustration
- Tapping or drumming fingers = Impatience
- Gaze down = Defeated attitude, guilt
- Hand to cheek = Evaluation, thinking
- Pinching bridge of nose, eyes closed = Negative evaluation
- Stroking chin = Trying to make a decision
- Rubbing hands = Anticipation
- Tilted head = Interest

Task 6.9

Video yourself teaching a session and spend time watching yourself and analysing your body language. What can you learn from this exercise?

Consequences

It is important to have consequences for poor behaviour. These consequences should be in line with your organization's discipline procedures and should be applied consistently and fairly to all situations.

Restorative justice

In the last ten years the application of the restorative justice philosophy and practice in school/college contexts has grown from isolated practice in individual organizations to a widespread initiative. Restorative justice means encouraging the young person to make amends or put things right when they have done something wrong. The growth in restorative justice suggests that educationalists introducing such approaches into schools/colleges are making significant progress in moving from retributive measures to restorative measures.

The intention of such people is not simply to change individuals' behaviour or provide closure for individual victims and their families, but to effect whole organization culture change, involving (but not limited to) the reform of an outmoded behaviour management policy based on sanctions and rewards.

While reduction in exclusion, improved behaviour and the satisfaction of those engaging in restorative meetings are important indicators of success, these are only part of the picture. There are other important measures of success such as an increased sense of safety; enhanced well-being and feeling of belonging; feeling listened to and respected; and improved self-esteem and resilience. All of these changes are observed not only in students but the whole school community.

In recent years the shift from a retributive mindset to a restorative mindset has been characterized by three main questions. Traditionally, by their own admission, in responding to a discipline incident, tutors/practitioners have first asked themselves:

- What happened? (the intention being to get to the bottom of the matter and establish 'the truth', and if necessary using interrogation techniques and witness statements);

- Who started it? (the intention being to identify the culprit, attribute guilt and assign blame);
- What needs to happen to deter and punish? (with the assumption that the threat of punishment acts as a deterrent and that the punishment itself ensures that the behaviour will not be repeated).

This contrasts very strongly with the way a restoratively-minded tutor would begin – which would be by asking themselves:

- I wonder what each person involved has experienced? (in other words, what has happened from each of their perspectives?)
- I wonder who has been affected by what has happened and how each person has been affected?
- I wonder how those affected can be supported in finding a way forward for themselves and repairing the harm?

We can see from this that the focus of restorative justice approaches is to involve participants in 'putting it right' and understanding the consequences of their behaviour. Used alongside measures already discussed, we can try to work towards eliminating re-offending and creating a culture of caring and supporting all learners.

Why do students misbehave?

It is, of course, important to accept that sometimes learners just want to be naughty and will behave badly despite our best efforts. For a minority of learners, it is easier to achieve status among their peers by anti-social conduct than through exerting the discipline required to be successful. However, tutors have a possible advantage in that they are not usually seen as the enemy by this group, unlike the police and other authorities. Tutors represent a 'softer' authority, and have a role in promoting socially acceptable behaviour within the college (Steward 2006).

The five key reasons that students' cite for their poor behaviour in the classroom are:

1 boredom
2 peer pressure
3 motivation
4 personality
5 opportunity.

If we look at each of these individually we can begin to consider some strategies to combat them.

Boredom

> Life is never boring, but some people choose to be bored
>
> (Wayne Dyer)

Most people blame boredom on the circumstances, but psychologists say this state is highly subjective and that levels of boredom vary among people. Some individuals are considerably more likely to be bored than others and this is particularly true of young people.

Boredom is not a unified concept but may comprise several varieties, including the transient type that occurs while waiting for a train and so-called existential boredom that accompanies a profound dissatisfaction with life. Boredom is linked to both emotional factors and personality traits. Problems with attention also play a role, and thus techniques that improve a person's ability to focus may diminish boredom.

For example, in a quiet classroom, you begin a frustrating fight against fatigue. The overhead projector hums, and you cannot concentrate on the slides. You stop absorbing information and doodle mindlessly. The tutor lost you ages ago. You are bored. Virtually everyone gets bored once in a while. Most of us chalk it up to a dull environment; however this does not need to be the case. We, the tutors can choose not to provide a 'dull environment'.

There are lots of reasons why students might be bored. The most common one is that they have no idea what to do. But other reasons might be they feel lazy or tired and just don't want to do the things that are available for them to do. Maybe they aren't feeling lazy, but they don't feel that they can do the things you want them to do.

Try the following top ten boredom busters:

1   Get active – use brain gym or some type of activity to get students moving around the room.
2   Get creative – do an activity that they have never done before.
3   Get busy – quicken up the pace of your session, time activities and give rewards.
4   Get focused – use short intense activities that require deep thought or quick responses.
5   Get humorous – bring humour into your sessions.
6   Get loud – use music as a background to activities.
7   Get messy – do activities that use a range of resources; young people like getting messy.
8   Get competitive – use competition to engage students.
9   Get interactive – use interactive activities to check learning.

10 Get challenging – raise the level of challenge in some activities to push the most able learners.

Peer pressure

Peer pressure is a term used to describe the pressure exerted by a peer group in encouraging a person to change their attitude, behaviour or morals, to 'fit in' with a particular group. While people are involved in this process of fitting in, they fail to see the consequences that are likely to occur from giving in to peer pressure. Young people fail to realize that negative peer pressure not only erodes their own identity but is also the sole reason for some of the poorest choices they make in their lives. Here are some facts about peer pressure:

- Peer pressure is the psychological force exerted by another, or others, of equal standing, which often influences a person into acting or behaving in a manner that is generally inconsistent with their normal behaviour.
- Peer pressure is most common in students of impressionable age or adolescents, but can also be cited at later stages in life.
- Peer pressure is not always negative. There are negative and positive effects of peer pressure. Peer pressure can be positive if the peers help in changing the person for better.
- Peer pressure can tend to have a very influential effect on the individuality of adolescents by influencing their choices in terms of movies, music, fashion and their way of life in general.
- Peer pressure can hamper the normal development and growth of a young person. This is a serious issue for you as tutors/practitioners in schools and colleges.
- Young people often fail to realize that they are getting into trouble and making choices as a result of peer pressure alone.
- Peer pressure is sometimes cited as one of the main reasons for unhealthy habits as well as deadly addictions like smoking, drinking and drug abuse.
- Peer pressure can also lead to involvement in unprotected sex and other harmful sexual acts and to issues like teen pregnancy.
- Peer pressure can be overcome with some help from tutors/practitioners, friends and family, but only with the commitment of the young person.

Why do people give into peer pressure? The main reason, and the reason given by most young people these days, is the need for belonging. This is part of Abraham Maslow's hierarchy of needs. In essence, it states that our motivations are dictated primarily by the circumstances we find ourselves in, and that certain 'lower' needs need to be satisfied before we are motivated towards 'higher' accomplishments. Within every human being there exists a hierarchy of five needs:

1 physiological
2 safety
3 social
4 esteem
5 self-actualization.

As each becomes substantially satisfied the individual moves up to the next step. We all have a desire to fit in and to be accepted and this is part of Maslow's need for social belonging. However, we often look for acceptance in groups that work against our achievement of success.

Here are some other reasons that we have come across which explain why young people give in to peer pressure; they are less known but equally valid:

- the lack of self-confidence to go their own way;
- the desire to avoid embarrassment;
- the lack of unbiased information;
- the need to conform, not to look different;
- the lack of clarity of their own views and opinions.

So how can we as tutors/practitioners overcome this pressure? Use the following top ten peer pressure busters:

1 Provide young people with witty responses to requests from their peers.
2 Provide young people with information and statistics.
3 Provide a safe environment.
4 Provide a reason to be 'good'.
5 Provide encouragement to the leader of the peer group to behave well and 'lead' the rest of the group.
6 Provide clear guidance and support.
7 Provide an uncritical environment where young people can come for advice about peer pressure.
8 Provide opportunities to gain acceptance from other groups of learners.
9 Provide praise and encouragement.
10 Provide a no tolerance policy to negative peer pressure.

Motivation

> Motivation is the willingness to exert high levels of effort toward goals, conditioned by the effort's ability to satisfy some individual need.
>
> (Abraham Maslow)

For years, managers, psychologists and academics have been interested in theories about motivation. Why we get out of bed and go to work every morning; why some people are willing to do a great job despite being faced with huge challenges on a daily basis; why others can't do even the simplest thing without making mistakes; and why seemingly small things such as the removal of a water-cooler in the canteen can have hugely detrimental effects on work performance.

Abraham Maslow's hierarchy of needs

Maslow's theory of the hierarchy of needs is probably the best-known motivation theory. It was developed by Abraham Maslow during the 1940s and 1950s. In essence, it states that our motivations are dictated primarily by our circumstances and that certain 'lower' needs need to be satisfied before we are motivated towards 'higher' accomplishments. As we explained above, the hierarchy consists of five needs and as each becomes substantially satisfied the individual moves up to the next step.

Task 6.10

- Next to each need in the hierarchy write an explanation of what it means to you.
- Using your students as an example, identify what they might need at each level to learn.

All the popular motivation theories have their flaws and detractors, but they do give us an insight into some of the mechanisms at work in day-to-day life. A number of key messages ring true: first, people are not automatons and their reasons for behaving in a certain way are more complex than just money or laziness. Secondly, different people are motivated differently – there is no such thing as a simple, all-encompassing solution. Thirdly, it's important to get the work environment right if you want to get the most from people; and finally, managing perceptions and expectations is very important if you want to help people get the most from their work.

Task 6.11

- List five things that motivate you at work.
- List five things that motivate you at home.
- Identify ten factors that might motivate students.

The following factors have been identified as influencing learner motivation:

Attitude of tutors/practitioners

1. patience;
2. open-mindedness;
3. friendliness;
4. enthusiasm for teaching;
5. balanced sense of humour;
6. understanding of young people and a readiness to discuss and help with their problems;
7. lack of arrogance;
8. recognition of own limitations;
9. a willingness to answer learners' questions;
10. a positive approach.

Treatment of learners

1. helpfulness;
2. avoidance of sarcasm;
3. not embarrassing learners before the class;
4. no ridiculing learners' questions or points of view;
5. giving full directions to learners and not expecting them to read one's mind;
6. firm, fair and impartial treatment.

Classroom practices

1. speaking to class instead of the board;
2. using good speaking techniques;
3. freedom from annoying mannerisms;
4. good chalkboard techniques;
5. attention to physical environment, for example seating arrangements, ventilation;
6. good sound session-planning with clearly stated objectives.

Personal appearance

1   appropriate dress;
2   appropriate hairstyles.

Grading and testing practice that influences motivation

1   grading in a consistent manner;
2   granting grades which are fair;
3   grading that is a real measure of the learner's achievement and knowledge *in the course,* not a measure of irrelevant factors;
4   giving tests/exams which are fair and free from gimmicks (tricks);
5   giving tests of reasonable length;
6   devising questions which are truly representative of material covered in class and reflect subject/course objectives.

Techniques to strengthen motivation

1   The individual learner's motivations and goals should be understood.
2   'Goals that are too hard or too easy to attain are neither motivating nor reinforcing when attained' (Bower and Hilgard 1981).
3   Short-term goals should be explained in relation to long-term achievement.
4   Sessions should be planned by the tutor and seen by the learner as part of a sequence eventually leading to the attainment of desirable ends.
5   Tasks should be appropriate to learners' abilities.
6   Attainment of competence should be explained in relation to higher levels of achievement.
7   Session material should be presented with enthusiasm and be meaningful to the learners.
8   Communication during the session should be pitched at a level which can be understood.
9   The fatigue which accompanies boredom should be avoided by planning a variety of techniques and activities.
10   A variety of motivating techniques should be used and the tutor should be aware of the differing levels of aspiration among the learners.
11   Assimilation of session material ought to be tested regularly.
12   Evaluation of test results should be conveyed to the learners as quickly as possible.
13   Competence should be recognized and reinforced by praise.
14   Temporary failure should be considered by the learner and the tutor as an occasion for a fresh attempt to overcome difficulties.

15 The tutor should build a relationship with students by treating them as individuals. It is important to smile and greet students as they enter the room.

16 The tutor should believe students can succeed – and give them hope.

17 A pleasant and stimulating learning environment should be created, including students' work on the walls.

18 The tutor must find something unique and positive about each student and point it out to them. They should take an interest in the student's outside activities.

19 From doing their PLRs, action plans and reviews, tutors should find out what a student's personal goals are, their hopes and dreams.

20 The tutor must enable the student to see their personal goal and then their goal on their course and help and involve them in planning for that goal.

21 The tutor must speak to students informally as they go round groups or workshops, or formally in one-to-one situations (tutorials).

22 Students should be encouraged to set goals and short term achievable targets, for example, 'I will have full attendance next week'.

23 Students should be provided with an element of choice by letting them select an activity or topic to research, and/or allowing them to choose how to demonstrate their understanding.

24 The tutor can invite students to help them solve classroom problems.

25 Honest, frequent, objective feedback with praise and recognition of effort and attainment should be provided.

26 The tutor should recognize accomplishments formally and informally.

27 Interesting, challenging and varied work should be provided.

28 The tutor should develop a culture of shared responsibility.

29 The tutor should show the student that they like them!

Personality

Every young person is developing their own personality and each will be different. They are going through a period of change and, as discussed in Chapter 1, are trying on a number of different personalities to see which one suits them. They may show evidence of multiple personalities depending upon who is teaching them and which other students are present.

An example of this is recounted by a colleague. She was having a really hard time with a student in her class and was having a 'moan' about him in the staff room only to have other colleagues say 'but he's lovely for me' and 'he's no trouble at all in my lessons'. She began to reflect on the situation and realized that she was experiencing a personality clash with the student which was as much her fault as his. When she came to understand this, she was able as a mature adult to put aside her natural response to him and, using emotional intelligence, was able to empathize with his position and they developed a strong working relationship. As she explained: 'I never came to like him, but I understood him and was able to get the best out of him. I don't think he ever knew I did not like him!'

We can see from this story that personality is an important factor in our relationships with students, both our own personalities and theirs. Sometimes certain characteristics 'put our backs up' but this is often because of other experiences in our own lives and not necessarily the student themselves. The key to dealing with different personalities is to take the time to reflect on what makes them tick and adjust our way of dealing with them accordingly. Many tutors will say they like teaching particular groups of students. For example, boys, girls, level 1 learners, level 3 learners, learners with additional needs. What they often mean is they deal better with these types of personality than they do with others. Becoming self-aware and challenging ourselves to work with learners that we do find difficult will make us better practitioners and will make us more understanding of diversity in our classrooms.

Opportunity

When asked why they have been 'naughty,' students will often say it was because they had the opportunity. An example of this was again told to me by a colleague. He had run out of handouts and had left the class to go and photocopy more. He was out of the room for only a few minutes, but on his return he found that one of the students had managed to put his hand through the window and had cut himself very badly. The student went to hospital and had a number of stitches and subsequently sued the college for not ensuring his health and safety. The member of staff was disciplined for leaving students unattended. We can see from this example that by giving the students the opportunity to misbehave, then that is often what they will do.

As tutors we need to make sure that we never give students that opportunity by allowing no spare time in our lessons. By keeping them busy and engaged we will avoid situations like the one above. It is often our most able students who misbehave through opportunity as they are the ones who are likely to have finished the work early and have nothing to do. By making sure we always have extension tasks for these learners we will minimize their opportunity to misbehave.

Syndromes and conditions

We should also consider that many of our learners will have additional learning needs that may or may not be diagnosed. The most common syndromes and conditions you will come across are outlined below.

Asperger's Syndrome

Asperger's Syndrome is one of the autistic spectrum disorders. A person with Asperger's Syndrome will have difficulties in communication, socialization and imagination, and sometimes physical coordination. The disorder is characterized by difficulty with social interaction, the development of restricted and repetitive patterns of behaviour, interests and activities.

Behaviours:

1 limited use of eye contact;
2 little social interaction and response;
3 lack of sharing;
4 failure to develop peer relationships;
5 no delay in development of spoken language;
6 inflexible adherence to routine and rituals;
7 preoccupation with one or a few areas of interest;
8 self critical and easily stressed.

Autism

Autism is developmental disability, affecting the communication and social skills of a person beyond the length of normal development. The triad of impairments identifies three areas in which development is delayed: social interaction, communication and restricted and repetitive patterns of behaviour.

Autism is a lifelong condition. Some autistic people are remarkably gifted in certain areas.

Behaviours:

1 limited use of eye contact;
2 little social interaction and response;

3   lack of sharing;
4   failure to develop peer relationships;
5   delay in development of spoken language;
6   inflexible adherence to routine and rituals;
7   preoccupation with one or a few areas of interest.

Attention deficit hyperactivity disorder (ADHD)

Attention deficit hyperactivity disorder is seen as a developmental disorder, causing emotional and behavioural difficulties. There are three main categories of ADHD: hyperactivity, impulsivity and inattention. People with ADHD can function well in casual settings. However they can find highly structured and less flexible environments, like colleges, extremely challenging.

Behaviours:

1   fidgeting;
2   talking continually;
3   struggling to partake in activities quietly;
4   difficulties concentrating/paying attention;
5   easily distracted/forgetful;
6   difficulties in waiting for their turn;
7   interruption of or intrusion on peers;
8   trouble with organizing activities.

Dyslexia

Dyslexia affects the way the brain processes written material. There are two types of dyslexia:

- acquired – skills affected as a result of illness or accident;
- developmental – child born with dyslexia and thus experiencing. difficulties with development of language and reading skills.

Young people with dyslexia struggle with spelling, grammar, sentence construction, telling left from right and many other issues.

Behaviours:

1   fidgeting;
2   talks continually;
3   struggles to partake in activities quietly;
4   has difficulties concentrating/paying attention;
5   easily distracted/forgetful;
6   has difficulties in waiting for their turn;

7   often interrupts or intrudes on peers;
8   has trouble with organizing activities.

Dyspraxia

Dyspraxia is a developmental coordination disorder. A person with dyspraxia will have some form of motor or sensory impairments, resulting in difficulties in coordination. It can be a result of some form of brain damage, or caused through delayed neurological development.

Behaviours:

1   poor balance;
2   trouble with hand–eye coordination;
3   difficulties with typing, handwriting and drawing;
4   poor at physical activities;
5   poor sense of direction;
6   frequently late;
7   concentration issues.

Dyscalculia

Dyscalculia is a condition affecting a person's ability to understand, remember and use numbers. It is a condition that affects the ability to acquire arithmetical skills. Dyscalculia learners may have difficulty understanding simple number concepts, lack an intuitive grasp of numbers and have problems learning number facts and procedures.

Behaviours:

1   low self esteem;
2   trouble with maths calculation;
3   phobia of maths;
4   difficulty in spelling and handwriting;
5   unable to tell the time;
6   unable to tell left from right.

Oppositional defiant disorder (ODD)

Oppositional defiant disorder is seen as an ongoing pattern of disobedient, hostile, and defiant behaviour towards authority figures, such as parents and teachers. People with ODD are continually defiant, and don't like taking orders from others. Five to 15 per cent of all school-age children have ODD.

Behaviours:

1   loses temper;
2   argues with adults;
3   refuses to follow rules;
4   deliberately annoys people;
5   blames others for own mistakes;
6   has anxiety/depression;
7   often irritable.

Obsessive compulsive disorder (OCD)

Obsessive compulsive disorder is an anxiety related disorder in which people are distressed by or limited in everyday functioning by obsessions and compulsions. They have no control over certain thoughts, ideas and urges. These can often be frightening or distressing or seem so unacceptable that the sufferer cannot share them with other people.

Behaviours:

1   fear of contamination;
2   excessive doubts;
3   preoccupation with detail, rules, lists, order;
4   rigidity;
5   stubbornness;
6   checking things over and over;
7   symmetry/ordering.

Tourette's syndrome

Tourette's syndrome is an inherited neurological disorder. The main identifying factors are multiple motor (body) ticks or vocal (phonic) ticks. These ticks are very difficult to control, getting better and worse over time, and cause distress and anxiety to the person.

Behaviours:

1   swearing for no reason;
2   hissing;
3   shouting;
4   repeating what people say;
5   head jerking/twitching;
6   defiant behaviour towards authority;

7 quick to lose temper;
8 sensitive to light, heat, and so on;
9 poor memory.

Task 6.12

Take each one of these syndromes and conditions in turn and think about the types of teaching strategies you would need to employ.

Case study 6.4: Wayne

Wayne joined the college in September 2006. When he was interviewed his mother stated that he had no identified special needs and had received no support at school. She was very forceful and gave Wayne little chance to speak for himself. In retrospect I feel that Wayne's mother felt guilty about his condition and tried to hide it in order that he be accepted as a 'normal' student. I believe she did not want him to have support believing he would be better off by not being singled out as 'different'. He had only passed one GCSE, grade A, in Religious Studies but had passed two vocational GCSE programmes in Business Studies and Leisure and Tourism, each of these being equivalent to two GCSEs. The opportunity for Wayne to take vocational programmes that did not have the same need for examinations and testing, and that related to his narrow field of interest, meant that he achieved the necessary entry criteria for the programme.

As the interviewer I was aware that there was something unusual about Wayne. He was reluctant to make eye contact and seemed remote and disengaged with the interview process. I now realize this was because of his Asperger's syndrome. As Wayne met the entry criteria of 5 Grade C GCSE passes and had already studied and passed a leisure and tourism course it was agreed that he would be accepted onto the programme and would undertake a diagnostic assessment in maths and literacy.

Before the start of the programme Wayne's mother was in contact on a number of occasions to check arrangements, and as a team we were beginning to be concerned and were prepared for an overprotective mother and a very spoiled young man. The induction programme for travel and tourism is all about team building and is very lively and fun. It culminates in a full 'fun day' with all classes competing against each other in a range of team games and sports. It became obvious on day one that Wayne was not

(continued)

going to be able to participate in all the activities. He appeared to shrink away from human contact and seemed not to know how to make friends.

Although we had never had a student with autism or any similar condition before, we were concerned enough to contact Wayne's parents and arrange for him to undertake an assessment with our leaning support department. Wayne was diagnosed with having Asperger's syndrome, dyslexia and dyspraxia. It also came to light that he suffers from panic attacks in group settings (especially exams). As a result of this diagnosis Wayne was allocated a one-to-one support worker in class. However as time went on we realized that Wayne was sinking and was not able to cope in his lessons. Nor was he able to cope with the constant change of lessons and the lesson content. Wayne was particularly struggling in his key skills lessons and in his resort rep lesson. On reflection this was probably because the key skills were working towards exams and the resort rep lessons are very practical and based on teamwork and communication skills.

At a team meeting we discussed whether we should modify his learning programme or fail him. However in PCET it is not that simple. Changing his programme of study affects the funding and the success rates of the department and the college. As such it is absolutely not permitted. It was decided to take this forward and try to make the changes that would help him succeed. This type of intervention was unusual but after many discussions It was agreed that Wayne would be able to take the course over three years rather than the standard two and would be able to drop the key skills and the resort reps qualifications. It was obvious that Wayne was much happier with the reduced programme and settled into a routine in his classes.

His support continued to be a problem as his support worker was constantly being changed and he was unable to make a continuous relationship with one person. Unexpected change is an area of difficulty for Wayne and many Asperger's sufferers. There is a routine established where they meet certain staff during their day and they can become very anxious when any change to that timetable occurs. The lack of explanation for that change is upsetting and disorientating for the student.

Wayne also had some problems making friends and understanding who his friends were. An example of this was when a group of students in his class put a dustbin on his head and were laughing as he ran around the room bumping into the desks. Wayne was not upset by this because he thought that they were laughing because they were his friends, although the teaching team was furious. As a result of this we decided to talk to the rest of the class in Wayne's absence and explain a little bit about Asperger's syndrome and Wayne's difficulties. At the start of the course we had decided not to do this, because we felt that it might draw attention to him and make him 'special'. However we were so appalled by their behaviour that we decided to talk to them as adults and to expect them to behave better in the future.

As a department we practise behaviour-for-learning techniques and believe in rewarding good behaviour not punishing bad, so we explained what Wayne's difficulties were and allowed them to discuss and question so as to be certain that they understood. We asked them to try and identify how they would feel if he was their brother and other people treated him like that. We finished the meeting by saying how disappointed we were about the incident and how we expected them to try and be his friends in the future. This tactic worked very well and he had no further problems with his classmates.

Another key incident in the first year was the residential visit to Brussels. After long discussion we decided to take Wayne's main support worker with us, as there were only five staff and fifty-six students and we felt we could not give him the one-to-one attention he needed. In hindsight this was not a good decision as it singled him out again and he hated it. Also his support worker thought she was on holiday and didn't look out for him. The students were able to have free time during the evening and Wayne wanted to be with the other students and not with the staff but it was very hard for us to trust them to look out for him as he is easily distracted and not easy to persuade. However the students had taken on board our discussions and were great and kept us informed.

The trip was not without incident however. On one occasion we were counting them on to the bus and said 'Where's Wayne?' The students said he was waiting round the corner because we had said they must meet us at the bus at 9.00am on the dot. Because he takes everything you say literally he was afraid to come back before the time and they could do nothing to persuade him. This was our mistake as we knew of this likely reaction and did not think before speaking.

On another occasion he got separated from his group and was lost. We were frantically looking for him and eventually found him back where we had started out. He had gone back to the place he had last seen us. He was not at all upset as he seemed to have no understanding that he was lost and was sure that we would be where he had left us. It had become obvious to us fairly early in the course that Wayne had some savant tendencies, a rare condition in which the person has areas of outstanding competence in certain subjects. Wayne had a phenomenal interest in travel geography and could place anywhere on a map without the use of an atlas. He absolutely loved knowing where places were and seemed to love the attention gained

(continued)

from getting it right. This soon attracted the admiration of his peers and he became accepted into the group more.

His tutor also started to set him challenges and entered him for a travel geography exam. This was a big move for Wayne because of his previous problems with exams. However he was allowed to take it on his own with a special invigilator. He passed this exam with 100 per cent and achieved another milestone in his learning journey. Wayne has since progressed onto the third year of his programme and is considering university. The planning for Wayne's transition to university has already started, with detailed reports being prepared and meetings being held with his parents and support workers.

Teaching strategies

We need to adjust our teaching strategies to meet the needs of these complex learners and you should consider using some of the following:

1 Adopt a multisensory approach to teaching.
2 Keep instructions short.
3 Plan small achievable targets.
4 Build self-esteem.
5 Focus on the positive and praise often.
6 Be calm and quiet and, above all, patient.
7 Use visual learning aids.
8 Avoid unstructured time.
9 Develop strategies to help them relax.
10 Allow time out in a safe zone.
11 Create structure and clear boundaries.
12 Make behaviour expectations clear.
13 Develop an appropriate support team.
14 Use ICT.

These techniques should work with most learners although you should always check their learning support plan and get expert advice where possible.

Chapter summary

The aim of this chapter is to focus on the learners and their specific needs and behaviours. Rather than focusing on their 'bad' behaviour we plan for their 'good' behaviour. Whatever the subject we teach, the needs and interests of these learners will remain the same and our ability to understand them, empathize with their issues and concerns, and enhance their learning, will be paramount in developing our teaching and their learning. By understanding the types of behaviour we are likely to meet and by identifying with learners' issues and concerns we can help them to succeed in becoming active citizens and valuable members of society.

Further reading

Kidd, W. and Czerniawski, G. (2010) *Successful Teaching 14–19: Theory, Practice and Reflection.* London: Sage.

Ogunleye, J. (2007) *Guide to Teaching 14–19.* London: Continnuum.

7   Final thoughts

What is this chapter about?

This chapter draws together the key themes covered in the previous chapters as well as introducing four new ones which will impact on all tutors who are involved in 14–19 learning and teaching. These are safeguarding, continuous professional development (CPD), experiential learning and quality assurance. The first two consider the wider social implications of managing 14–19 learning and the need to support and promote outstanding tutors in the sector. The latter two draw upon concepts explored in Chapters 2 and 5 and give food for thought as you consider the application of all the ideas which have been recommended in this book to your own professional context.

Task 7.1 Preliminary reading

Wood, J. and Dickinson, J. (2011) *Quality Assurance and Evaluation in the Lifelong Learning Sector.* Exeter: Learning Matters.

Safeguarding

Safeguarding is about protecting children and vulnerable adults from maltreatment, preventing impairment to health or development, and promoting welfare to create opportunities to enable optimum life chances. Some facts to think about:

- Abuse happens regardless of gender, age, ability, race or culture.
- Abusers are most likely to be known and trusted by those they abuse.
- Children/young people very rarely lie about or exaggerate abuse.

- We all have a duty to safeguard children and should never promise confidentiality; the law is clear – we have a duty to share information to keep children and vulnerable adults safe.

How has current safeguarding legislation come about?

There are four key cases that have lead to the current legislative situation.

1 Victoria Climbié (2000)

Victoria Climbié was known to four social services departments, two police child protection teams, two hospitals, two housing offices, one homeless persons unit, one child and family centre, one practice nurse, two health visitors, one teacher, two baptist ministers, one unregistered childminder and one taxi driver (who took Victoria to hospital before she died) and yet she died as a result of horrific abuse. Her death led to the Lord Laming enquiry, which in turn led to the Every Child Matters Agenda in the Children Act (2004). As a result of this, guidance was given to agencies on how to work together and this led to the Common Assessment Framework.

2 Lauren Wright (2001)

Lauren Wright was a significant case because she died from parental abuse while attending school regularly. The result of this case was that Safeguarding Children in Education came into being in the Education Act 2002. This made it our responsibility as tutors/practitioners to report all concerns about children, young people and vulnerable adults to the designated person, who MUST take action.

3 Holly Wells and Jessica Chapman (2002)

This case was significant because Ian Huntley worked in a school and was in a position of trust with children. He had also worked in other areas of the country where concerns had been raised, but no charges had been made. This led to the Bichard Report. This report made 31 recommendations, the most significant of which was the introduction of a compulsory registration scheme for all people working in education. This scheme would result in a list of people barred from working with children, young people and vulnerable adults and would be shared with all institutions in the sector. At the time of going to press this scheme has yet to be implemented.

4 Baby P (2008)

The death of Baby P in 2008 was significant because it once again threw the spotlight on safeguarding. In spite of all the preceding legislation and reports, Baby P, who was known to social services as being at risk, died from neglect and abuse. This led to *The Protection of Children in England – A Progress Report*, which attempted to tighten up safeguarding legislation.

What is current legislation?

Section 175 of the Education Act 2002 (came into force June 2004)

This requires LEAs and governing bodies of schools and FE institutions to make arrangements to ensure that their functions are carried out with a view to safeguarding the welfare of children, young people and vulnerable adults.

Safeguarding Children in Education (September 2004)

This provides guidance on the duties of schools and FE institutions with respect to having arrangements in place to safeguard and promote the welfare of children, young people and vulnerable adults. It is now a statutory requirement to have regard to guidance issued. The guidance requires governing bodies to undertake an annual review of the safeguarding policies and procedures and how these duties have been discharged. The governing body also has a responsibility to remedy any weaknesses with respect to the school's/college's safeguarding arrangements which are brought to its attention.

Working Together to Safeguard Children/Young People (2006)

This provides statutory guidance on the roles and responsibilities of agencies working together to safeguard children/young people. In addition it sets out the framework for the formation of Local Safeguarding Children Boards and also details the allegation management process.

What do we mean by abuse?

There are seven key categories of abuse. These are:

1. **Physical abuse** may involve hitting, shaking, throwing, poisoning, burning or scalding, drowning, suffocating, or otherwise causing physical harm. Physical harm may also be caused to a

child when a parent/carer fabricates the symptoms of, or deliberately induces, illness.

2 **Neglect** is the persistent failure to meet basic medical, physical and/or psychological needs, likely to result in the serious impairment of health or development. It may involve:
   - failing to provide access to appropriate health, social care or education services;
   - failing to provide adequate nutrition, clothing, heating or shelter, including exclusion from home or abandonment;
   - failing to protect from physical harm or danger;
   - failing to ensure adequate care or supervision (including the use of inadequate carers);
   - neglect of, or lack of responsiveness to, basic emotional needs.
      Neglect may also occur to an unborn child during pregnancy as a result of maternal substance misuse.

3 **Sexual abuse** involves forcing or enticing a young person or vulnerable adult to take part in sexual activities, including prostitution, whether or not they are aware of what is happening. The activities may involve physical contact, including penetrative acts or non-penetrative acts. They may include non-contact activities such as looking at or involvement in the production of online sexual material, watching sexual activities, or encouraging inappropriate sexual behaviour.

4 **Emotional abuse** is persistent emotional mal-treatment such as to cause severe and persistent adverse effects on emotional development or well-being. It may involve:
   - conveying that the young person is worthless or unloved, inadequate, or valued only insofar as they meet the needs of another person;
   - age or developmentally inappropriate expectations. These may include interactions that are beyond developmental capabilities, as well as overprotection and limitation of exploration and learning, or preventing participation in normal social interaction;
   - serious bullying, causing a young person or vulnerable adult to frequently feel frightened or in danger;
   - the exploitation or corruption of a child, young person or vulnerable adult.

   In addition to definitions provided above, in the context of vulnerable adults the following definitions apply:

5 **Psychological abuse** including emotional abuse, threats of harm or abandonment, deprivation of contact, humiliation, blaming, controlling, intimidation, coercion, harassment, verbal

abuse, isolation, or withdrawal from services or supportive networks.

6 **Financial or material abuse** including theft, fraud, exploitation, pressure in connection with wills, property or inheritance
or financial transactions, or the misuse or misappropriation of
property, possessions or benefits.

7 **Discriminatory abuse** including racist and sexist abuse or harassment, abuse or harassment based on disability or other forms
of harassment, slurs or similar treatment.

Task 7.2

Have you undergone safeguarding training? If not make sure you attend a
session.

Make yourself familiar with the safeguarding policy and procedure of
your organization.

What is your responsibility?

The increased focus on safeguarding in education has led to a much greater
role for the tutor/practitioner in looking out for signs of abuse/neglect
in young people and vulnerable adults and in reporting those concerns
to the designated safeguarding officer in your organization. Where your
concerns relate to 14–16-year-old learners who come to you from a school
you need to inform the schoolteacher who accompanies them as well
as your own organization's designated safeguarding officer. We cannot
promise confidentiality to young people in these situations because we
have a legal and moral duty to protect them from harm, so we MUST
act on all information that we come across in the course of our work.
The designated safeguarding officer will ensure that the young person or
vulnerable adult is removed from harm's way and a full investigation is
carried out.

Continual professional development (CPD)

Here we explore the concept of dual professionalism, the status of
Qualified Teacher Learning and Skills (QTLS) and the need for all tutors
to engage in specific CPD in order to provide every learner with expert
tuition and meaningful learning experiences. First it would be useful to

review the history and role of the Institute for Learning (IfL), the new professional body for teachers and trainers in PCET.

The Institute for Learning (IfL)

The IfL was formed in 2002 by and for further education teachers and others, and is the professional body for teachers, tutors, trainers and student teachers in the further education and skills sector which includes adult and community learning, emergency and public services, FE colleges, the armed services, sixth form colleges, the voluntary and community sector and work-based learning. It mirrors the role of the GTC (General Teaching Council) which oversees the school sector. The IfL is an independent professional body governed by an elected advisory council which works closely with learning and skills organizations, unions and employer bodies (www.ifl.ac.uk 2010).

Since 2001, pedagogical debates and discourses within the PCET sector have embraced the development of shared aims and values within the professional setting. These initially lead to Further Education National Training Organisation (FENTO) endorsed qualifications (pre-2007) and latterly to Life Long Learning UK (LLUK) endorsed staged qualifications namely PTLLS (Preparing to Teach), CTLLS (Certificate to Teach), DTLLS (Diploma to Teach) otherwise known as PGCE/Certificate of Higher Education (see Box 7.1). These qualifications focus on 'generic' pedagogy and as such are created for use across the PCET sector. The subject specific elements are not taught; rather they are mentored in the workplace and researched by the trainee. This was, and is, an attempt to 're-professionalise a broad and diverse workforce. Statistically 40% of full time staff and 43% of part time staff in the PCET sector had no high level teaching certificate in 2003' (Armitage et al. 2003: 273) and many were and are vocationally oriented trainers, assessors and instructors whose teaching and training is grounded in the needs of the workplace. The 'generic' teaching qualification is now mandatory for all PCET employees and is available in various levels.

Box 7.1   **The LLUK qualifications**

Stage 1   PTTLS – Level 3/4
Stage 2   CTTLS – Level 4/5
Stage 3   DTTLS – Level 5/6/7

QTLS is the full status for qualified PCET teachers. It is not QTS (Qualified Teacher in Schools) and this is currently contested. The IfL's chief executive, Toni Fazaeli, said in an IfL press release (October 2010):

> Under current legislation, excellent teachers of vocational subjects in further education who hold the professional status of QTLS are not recognised as being able to teach in schools. When a school in England wants to expand its practical and applied learning for young people, but cannot recruit from among the best vocational teachers holding QTLS, something is wrong. (IfL October 2010)

This situation may be reviewed by the coalition government.

QTLS and CPD

In order to gain QTLS and be termed a fully qualified teacher as opposed to ATLS (associate teacher) one needs to meet the standards appropriate to each. A distinction is inferred here between teachers and trainers. Broadly, trainers apply for ATLS and teachers for QTLS although there is a great deal of debate on what an ATLS prospective trainer actually does.

In order to qualify as a teacher you must demonstrate high quality subject specific knowledge at the appropriate level as well as high quality pedagogical skills. This is termed Dual Professionalism (IfL 2010) and means that a professionally competent plumber, for example, is not necessarily a professionally competent teacher so the former should not, as was the case before 2001, be the automatic passport to becoming the latter. Continuing professional development in both subject specific skills and in pedagogical skills are of equal importance and it is therefore vital that tutors engage proactively with professional formation.

What is CPD?

Continuous Professional Development promotes the concept of dual professionalism. In other words it promotes the notion of experts in teaching and training methods as well as experts with up to date vocational or subject knowledge. CPD should be the focus of all professional activity and not simply a 'one off' event. The IfL have an excellent summary of what CPD should entail:

All tutors in the sector should:

1   Make time for reflective practice and critically analyse their own objectives. They build their confidence in their own professional judgement, tailoring learning activities

to individual students' and trainees' needs and circumstances.

2   Learn from others and are willing to share practice and engage in peer support, mentoring and collaborative action research, sharing, networking with other teachers and trainers and learning from others in communities of practice.

3   Require the support of leaders who are experts in learning and can prioritize improving teaching and learning. The best leaders set the tone for brilliant teaching and develop a culture of self-improvement.

4   Are expert at how to design and match teaching and training methods to learners' needs, the subject and level of programme. They have a wide repertoire of methods on which to draw and know which are most effective in what circumstances.

5   Continually listen and respond to learners, bringing enthusiasm and creativity to learning, monitoring progress and acting upon feedback. They recognize the importance of being a professional with a full commitment to the learner.

6   Are confident in their use of technology, inventive with different and emerging technologies to enhance the learning experience and successful learning.

7   Maximize use of virtual learning environments (VLEs) and online learning to build knowledge and become more effective teachers and trainers.

8   Are actively involved in assessment for learning and target-setting for learners.

9   Work with newly qualified teachers and trainers, and peers, to build discussion and reflective practice.

Brilliant teachers and trainers are **real experts in their subject area**, and they:

1   Work hard to maintain their occupational, specialist or subject knowledge.

2   Are passionate about their subject and do not feel it is a chore to teach it.

3   Build their own links with their appropriate professional institutions to keep up to date.

4   Engage in sector vocational or subject networks.

5   Continually develop and build links with employers, experts and higher education in related fields.

6   Spend time out in industry with employers for their own development.
7   Actively engage employers in the student or trainee learning experience.
8   Plan for the coherence of on- and off-the-job training in their vocational area.

(Available online at www.ifl .ac.uk (2010) Brilliant teaching and training in FE and skills: A guide to effective CPD for teachers, trainers and leaders)

Task 7.3

Review the previous section on what constitutes good CPD and draw up an action plan based on the following points:

- Review on your own what makes brilliant teachers and trainers and consider to what extent you engage in any of these activities.
- Discuss different CPD approaches and activities that work with colleagues and peers. Discuss aspects of brilliant teaching and training; would this be a valuable addition to your CPD over the next year?
- Reflect on what CPD you have done and what experience of CPD you could share.
- What are your new CPD priorities, and what help and support do you need from others?
- How do you integrate this into your current CPD and how can technology help you?

What are your options?

Graduate options

If you are already a graduate and a qualified teacher (either QTS or QTLS) then you might want to consider embarking upon a Masters degree in Education.

There are two types of Masters degrees available, there is the traditional taught programme and the practice-based route.

Taught programmes traditionally lead to a named pathway, for example: MA in Leadership and Management in Post Compulsory Education and Training or MA in 14–19 Education. These programmes consist of a variety of modules giving you 120 credits and a dissertation giving you a further 60 credits. It is normally possible to exit after 60 credits with a Postgraduate certificate or after 120 credits with a Postgraduate diploma.

Practice-based programmes are based around researching your own practice and submitting modules based on that research. These are normally assessed by the completion of a portfolio of evidence and a reflective piece of writing about the impact of the research on your own practice. The modules are much broader in nature as each student will be focusing on different aspects of their practice. These modules are not normally taught but are often supported by online tutors.

Accessing these programmes

Often your school/college/union or local authority will have a partnership with a university in order to access programmes at a discounted rates. It is always worth investigating this option first. You can also apply for staff development funding to help towards the cost of studying at this level. Information on courses will be on the website of each university and it is worth looking at a few to see what suits you best.

Non-graduate options

If you are not a graduate then your options are different. If you have a CertEd or similar teaching qualification then you can 'top' this up to a foundation degree and then progress on to a BA (Hons) degree.

Foundation degrees in Lifelong Learning or PCET are available at most universities and would entail either taught modules or online modules to be undertaken.

BA (Hons) degree programmes offer you a further chance to 'top' up to a full degree and include similar modules to those in the foundation degree and a dissertation based on your own practice.

CPD for other staff in schools and colleges

There are many other staff working in the 14–19 sector who are not teachers but who work closely with young people. There are many options available for accredited CPD including foundation degrees, degrees, CPD modules and practice-based research.

Task 7.4

Investigate what CPD is available to you via partnerships with universities.

Visit Edge Hill University and look at the range of options – www.edgehill. ac.uk – and compare this with another university. Does anything interest you?

Experiential learning

Experiential learning, sometimes known as participative learning, is a process which directly acknowledges, welcomes, values and uses the existing knowledge and competence of those being taught. Its use is particularly appropriate where the subject matter under consideration touches on people's deeply held beliefs and attitudes, involves emotionally charged or value-laden material, or is just plain difficult in human terms!

In this section we draw on Kolb's theory of experiential learning and its application in teaching. At the heart of this theory is the idea that learners' prior experiences and current knowledge can be used to implement effective learning. Kolb suggests that there are four stages of learning:

- concrete experience;
- observations and reflections;
- formation of abstract concepts and generalizations;
- testing the implications of concepts in new situations.

These stages form a cycle that you continue to follow in a spiral fashion in order to improve your practice.

Kolb, together with Fry (Kolb and Fry 1976), also developed a Learning Style Inventory which is designed to measure a learner's relative position on the 'concrete experience' versus 'abstract conceptualization' dimension and the 'active experimentation' versus 'reflective observation' dimension.

How can this model help tutors create positive attitudes to learning? It is possible to summarize the approaches as follows. In that of 'traditional teacher' the teacher is a deliverer of information with learners in rows, maybe taking notes. The 'modern tutor' is a facilitator, assisting learners to learn for themselves. Learners will be in groups, carrying out tasks and may not even be in the same building or could be at different stages of their learning.

Learners bring with them a wealth of experience. They are encouraged to plan and negotiate their own learning. Not everyone learns in the same manner, so just talking to or at learners might not be good for all. Not all learn at the same pace, or at the tutor's pace, so there is a need for some individualization. Learning is more effective when it is based on experiences. Therefore concepts are learnt better if acted out or practised. The tutor focuses on learners' current experiences and gives learners some responsibility for what is learnt. As explored earlier in Chapter 2, learning can take place in a variety of settings.

Task 7.5

- Identify the four key stages in experiential learning.
- Evaluate the implications of Kolb's theory and its application in teaching.
- Identify teaching strategies based on experiential learning theory which you can use in your own practice.

Experience, reflection and learning

As with the experiential learning model, the process of learning can be viewed as cyclical. In the classroom, tutors provide scenarios or experiences, but they must remember to also provide activity which ensures reflection and consolidates learning.

Scenarios and experiences can take the form of simulation, role play, practical tasks, watching a TV programme or even listening to a presentation. Activities for encouraging reflection include group discussions to share views, perceptions and ideas.

Experiential learning can involve practising particular skills, applying knowledge in a new situation and completing a written assignment with help from additional reading material.

Whatever the activity or setting, the prior knowledge and experiences of the learners will be the focus of the session.

Task 7.6

Use this approach to design a session plan making specific references to the experiential learning model.

The impact of experiential learning

Case study 7.1: Chris

As part of our studies we were invited to form our own teams to research an area and to experience working in teams. I joined a team with two others.

(continued)

According to Belbin's Team Role Theory (1981), there are eight primary roles in an effective team. These are governed by personality, work ethic, personal preferences and the task faced by the team. After around an hour's initial debate over the subject matter, I emerged as the shaper/coordinator and was informally 'elected' as group leader.

Tuckman (1965) proposed four principal phases in the development of a team from inception to full operational efficiency:

- **Forming** the selection/collation of individuals into a group.
- **Storming** the 'settling-in period', when (leader and) team members establish their relative positions and adapt to the group culture.
- **Norming** the end of the honeymoon period, when the team settles into a rhythm and is able to focus on tasks as a cohesive group.
- **Performing** when all team members naturally recognize the strategic vision, anticipate task needs and work efficiently together.

Because the team members were already well acquainted (and cordial), the first two phases were swifter and less traumatic than they might have been.

The formation was straightforward: on the surface, we enjoyed each other's company, sharing similar humour and interests. Although not explicit, I believe we automatically recognized that we had a good mixture of work ethic, personality and opinions. Two of us had worked together before, developing a teaching session on Multiple Intelligences (Gardner 1983). Again, there was unspoken recognition that we had a good blend of MI types: I am primarily a people person (intra/interpersonal); another is strong with logic and language; the third is artistic, enabling him to identify the kinaesthetic and affective aspects of our report.

As there was little need to establish a 'pecking order', I was able to maintain a participative/delegative style of coordination and leadership (Lewin et al. 1939). I could therefore delegate activities with my focus on the task and individual needs, rather than having to work on maintaining the team (Adair 1988). I set up a structure for ongoing discussion and coordination, based upon our attendance at university, supplemented by a structured email system: I set up one 'string' of emails for discussion of the subject matter and a second for administrative matters.

As with any project, we met with minor glitches – especially as 'B' met with difficulties at home during the project. Accordingly, we made dynamic changes to the timings, although the plan itself was largely unaffected. In practice, this meant that the time allocated from three weeks to five, leaving me with only a few days to finalize the document. This proved to be less traumatic than it may seem, as I prefer to give my complete attention to a single task, rather than spreading it over a long period; it simply meant, however, that there was little leeway, meaning that there was a very small 'safety net' if we disagreed over the final draft.

Conclusions

Our sequential approach certainly lent itself to cooperative experiential learning, although I think a more correct portrayal of our relationship would be: a learner-centred instructional process in which small intentionally se-lected groups of 3–5 students work interdependently on a well-defined learning task; individual students are held accountable for their own per-formance and the instructor serves as a facilitator/consultant in the group learning process (Cuseo 1992).

I think the defining word is 'interdependently', which emphasizes that we worked with supervision independently, but not in total isolation from each other's input and influence. In other words, we depended upon information from others to prepare and to inform the final draft and editing process. I certainly benefited from the experience: as the third person in the sequence, I was able to draw upon ideas and viewpoints that would not otherwise have occurred to me. As a strong-willed and single-minded person, I have also learned that cooperation and flexibility (especially in making room for the input of others) offers great advantages: in the cross-fertilization of ideas, as well as the division of labour.

This case study highlights the learning that has taken place by this student undertaking a project and then reflecting critically on it and its effect on himself as a learner. We can see that he has learnt a lot from this experience and will perhaps approach similar tasks differently in the future as a result of this reflective process.

Quality assurance looking to the future

As we saw at the beginning of this book, 14–19 education is a con-stantly changing sector and is at the mercy of government and legislative changes. The horizon is constantly changing and developing, although one focus of this and likely successive governments will be on the quality of provision and how this is maintained and improved.

It is a fundamental principle of the Quality Assurance System that providers remain responsible for delivering a high quality education for their learners. In doing this, they will need continually to review and assess their own performance and be proactive in improving the quality of education and training that they offer.

Central government, in consultation with sector bodies, will continue to set national minimum standards which providers are expected to meet. Until the Framework for Excellence (FfE) becomes fully embedded and implemented across the sector, the current approach to the setting, measurement and use of Minimum Levels of Performance (MLPs) will continue. Framework for Excellence results will in future be used to influence discussions about performance and standard setting.

When deciding whether or not to fund provision, lead commissioners will consider

- the needs of learners, employers and the local community;
- levels of demand and local demography;
- the need to make improvements to the quality of the sector, whilst still sustaining the viability of providers so that demand is met; and
- local, regional and national strategies, which will set priorities and available budgets.

Provider performance will be reviewed on an annual basis and, in conducting these reviews, sponsoring agencies and lead commissioners will take a range of evidence and information into account. The Annual Performance Assessment and subsequent actions will be proportionate to any issues or concerns that are raised. A good provider who is meeting the needs of learners and employers can expect a light touch assessment and little challenge. However, in cases where provision is not good enough or, at worst, inadequate, action will be taken quickly. An action plan will be agreed with the provider, outlining how any concerns will be addressed and quality delivery resumed. Failure to respond to this may lead to a withdrawal of funding or provision.

(Department for Business, Innovation and Skills 2010: 10)

We can see from this extract that there is a fundamental desire to increase the quality of provision in education and that those who do not improve will face serious consequences and funding issues.

At the time of going to press there are further revisions being made to the quality assurance processes used by government to monitor the quality of provision but it is clear that whatever mechanisms are chosen there will always be a strong focus on the quality of teaching and learning, the learners' experiences and the value for money provided by organizations.

Task 7.7

Get a copy of the latest Ofsted report for your organization.

What do they say about the quality of the teaching and learning, the student experience and the value for money offered?

Chapter summary

In this chapter we have raised some other issues for you to think about and discuss how they might impact on your experience of teaching in the sector. Due to the increasingly complex political situation and the never-ending change that the sector faces it is difficult to be certain about the future. However, safeguarding and quality assurance are issues that may change in the way they are implemented by successive governments but they are here to stay as a focus for making the sector and individual tutors/practitioners accountable for their actions and the effect of these actions on the lives of young people in their care.

By considering experiential learning and reflection we are encouraging you to reflect on your practice and to consider ways of improving to stay ahead of the game and maximize your impact on the lives of your students. Keeping up to date and undertaking CPD in order to improve your practice and gain additional qualifications adds to your marketability and to the quality of your teaching and learning. It may also give you the opportunity to progress within your organization or to move to another.

The role of the tutor/practitioner is a very complex and difficult one and it involves a huge number of skills and abilities. We hope that we have been able to address some of these in this book and to offer an insight into the complex area of 14–19 education. We wish you well and leave you with our view that this is a vocation and not just a job; it is a passion that takes over your life and may keep you awake at night worrying or preparing lessons, but is never boring, always interesting, and sometimes extremely moving.

Further reading

Armitage, A., Bryant, R., Dunhill, R. et al. (2007) *Teaching and Training in Post-Compulsory Education,* 3rd edn. Maidenhead: Open University Press.

Fairclough, M. (2008) *Supporting Learners in the Lifelong Learning Sector.* Maidenhead: Open University Press.

Steward, A. (2009) *Continuing your Professional Development in Lifelong Learning.* London: Continuum.

Bibliography

Adair, J. (1988) *The Action-Centred Leader*. London: Kogan Page.

Armitage, A., Bryant, R., Dunhill, R. et al. (2007) *Teaching and Training in Post-compulsory Education*, 3rd edn. Maidenhead: Open University Press.

Belbin, R.M. (1981) *Management Teams: Why They Succeed or Fail*. Portsmouth: Heinemann.

Belbin, R.M. (2010) *Belbin® Team Role Theory*. http://www.belbin.com/rte.asp?id=8 (accessed May 2010).

Boud, D. (1985) *Reflection: Turning Experience into Learning*. London: Routledge-Falmer.

Bower, G.H. and Hilgard, E.R. (1981) *Theories of Learning*. Englewood Cliffs, NJ: Prentice-Hall.

Clarke, S. (2005) *Formative Assessment in the Secondary Classroom*. London: Hodder Murray.

Clough, P. and Corbett, J. (2000) *Theories of Inclusive Education: A Student's Guide*. London: Sage.

Curnock Cook, M. (2010) http://www.ucas.ac.uk/about_us/media_enquiries/media_releases/2010/210110 (accessed 16 August 2011).

Curzon, L.B. (1990) *Teaching in FE*, 4th edn. London: Cassell.

Cuseo, J. (1992) Cooperative learning vs small group discussions and group projects: the critical differences. Cooperative Learning and College Teaching.

Department for Business, Innovation and Skills (2010) *The Quality Assurance System for Post-16 Education and Training Provision*. London: DCSF/BIS.

Dewey, J. (1938) *Experience and Education*. New York: Collier Macmillan.

Fawbert, F. (2008) *Teaching in Post-Compulsory Education: Skills, Standards and Lifelong Learning*. London: Continuum.

FEFC (1996) *Inclusive Learning: Report of the Learning Difficulties and/or Disabilities Committee*. London: HMSO.

Gardner, H. (1983) *Frames of Mind: Theory of Multiple Intelligences*. London: Harvard.

Gill, D. and Adams, B. (1989) *ABC of Communication Studies*. London: Macmillan.

Goleman, D. (1996) *Emotional Intelligence*. London: Bloomsbury.

Grandin, T. (2006) *Thinking in Pictures*. London: Bloomsbury.

Gravells, A. and Simpson, S. (2008) *Planning and Enabling Learning in the Lifelong Learning Sector*. Exeter: Learning Matters.

Hillier, Y. (2005) *Reflective Teaching in Further and Adult Education*, 2nd edn. London: Continuum.

Holloway, J. (2004) *Hidden Disabilities: The Teaching Kit*. Lewes: Connect Publications.

IFL (2010) Review of CPD. http://www.ifl.ac.uk/_data/assets/pdf_file/0005/17744/2011_01/IFL_review_of_epd_2009_10_for_web.pdf

Illeris, K. (2009) *Contemporary Theories of Learning*. Abingdon: Routledge.

Jordan, A., Carlile, O. and Stack, A. (2008) *Approaches to Learning*. London: Open University Press.

Kegan, R. (2009) What 'form' transforms, in K. Illeris (ed.) *Contemporary Theories of Learning*. Abingdon: Routledge, 35–52.

Keeley-Browne, L. (2007) *Training to Teach in the Learning and Skills Sector*. Essex: Pearson Education.

Kennedy, H. (1997) *Learning Works: Widening Participation in Further Education*. Coventry: FEFC/HMSO.

Knowles, M. (1973) *The Adult Learner: A Neglected Species*. Houston, TX: Gulf Publishing Company.

Knowles, M. (1980) *The Modern Practice of Adult Education: From Pedagogy to Andragogy*. Chicago, IL: Follett.

Knowles, M. (1984) *The Adult Learner: A Neglected Species*, 3rd edn. Houston, TX: Gulf Publishing Company.

Kolb, D.A. and Fry, R. (1975) Toward an applied theory of experiential learning, in C. Cooper (ed.) *Theories of Group Process*. London: Wiley.

Lea, J., Hayes, D., Armitage, A., Lomas, L. and Markless, S. (2003) *Working in Post-Compulsory Education*. Maidenhead: Open University Press.

Lefrancois, G.R. (1994) *Psychology for Teaching*, 8th edn. Belmont, CA: Wadsworth.

Lewin, K., Llippit, R. and White, R.K. (1939) Patterns of aggressive behavior in experimentally created social climates, *Journal of Social Psychology*, 10: 271–301.

Lumby, J. and Foskett, N. (2005) *14–19 Education: Policy, Leadership and Learning*. London: Sage.

Marshall, F. (2004) *Living with Autism*. London: Sheldon Press.

Mezirow, J. (2009) An overview on transformative learning, in K. Illeris (ed.) *Contemporary Theories of Learning*. Abingdon: Routledge, 90–106.

Moser, C. (1999) *A Fresh Start: Improving Literacy and Numeracy*. London: DfEE.

Petty, G. (2004) *Teaching Today*, 3rd edn. Cheltenham: Nelson Thornes.

Petty, G. (2010) *Teaching Today*, 4th edn. Cheltenham: Nelson Thornes.

Pring, R. (2000) *Philosophy of Educational Research*. London: Continuum.

Pring, R., Hayward, G., Hodgson, A. et al. (2009) *Education for All – The Future of Education and Training for 14–19-year-olds*. London: Routledge.

Race, P. (2005) *Making Learning Happen: A Guide for Post-Compulsory Education*. London: Sage Publications.

Reece, I. and Walker, S. (2007) *Teaching, Training & Learning*. Tyne & Wear: Business Education Publishers.

Roffey, S. (2004) *The New Teacher's Survival Guide to Behaviour*. London: Sage.

Rogers, A. (2002) *Teaching Adults*. Maidenhead: Open University Press.

Rogers, C.R. (1983) *Freedom to Learn for the 80s*. Columbus, OH: Merrill.

Rogers, J. (2007) *Adults Learning*, 5th edn. London: Open University Press.

Smith, A. (1996) *Accelerated Learning in the Classroom*. Stafford: Network Educational Press.

Steward, A. (2006) *A to Z of Teaching in FE*. London: Continuum.

Steward, A. (2008) *Getting the Buggers to Learn in FE*. London: Continuum.

Tomlinson, J. (1996) *Inclusive Learning: The Report of the Learning Difficulties and/or Disabilities Committee of the Further Education Funding Council*. London: HMSO.

Tredway, L. (1995) Socratic seminars: engaging learners in intellectual discourse, *Educational Leadership*, 53(1): 26–9.

Tuckman, B.W. (1965) Developmental sequence in small groups, *Psychological Bulletin*, 63: 384–99. (The article is available as a Word document: http://dennislearningcenter.osu.edu/references/GROUP%20 DEV%20ARTICLE.)

Tuckman, B., Abry, D. and Smith, D.R. (2001) *Learning and Motivation Strategies: Your Guide to Success*. Upper Saddle River, NJ: Prentice-Hall.

Vizard, D. (2007) *How to Manage Behaviour in Further Education*. London: Sage.

Wallace, S. (2007a) *Teaching, Tutoring and Training in the Lifelong Learning Sector*, 3rd edn. Exeter: Learning Matters.

Wallace, S. (2007b) *Managing Behaviour in the Lifelong Learning Sector*, 2nd edn. Exeter: Learning Matters.

Williams, R. and Pritchard, C. (2006) *Breaking the Cycle of Educational Alienation*. Maidenhead: Open University Press.

Index

CONTEMPORARY ISSUES IN LIFELONG LEARNING

Vicky Duckworth and Jonathan Tummons

9780335241125 (Paperback)
2010

eBook also available

This book provides an up-to-date and critical analysis of contemporary issues and debates in the lifelong learning sector (LLS) The themes are presented in an accessible format, and are underpinned by recent research as well as policy analysis. The authors examine significant issues in the LLS today including inclusive practice, the employability agenda, the curriculum in the LLS and research-led teaching.

Key features:

- Learning outcomes at the beginning of each chapter
- Links to QTLS standards
- Case studies

www.openup.co.uk

OPEN UNIVERSITY PRESS
McGraw - Hill Education

SUPPORTING LEARNERS IN THE LIFELONG LEARNING SECTOR

Marilyn Fairclough

978-0-335-23362-5 (Paperback)
2008

eBook also available

This is the first book of its kind to deal with the topic of *supporting* learners in PCET, rather than just focusing on how to teach them.

Key features:

- Each chapter cross-referenced to the QTLS Professional Standard for those on PTLLS, CTLLS and DTLLS courses
- Real life examples from a variety of settings and subjects
- Practical suggestions for developing classroom practice
- Suggestions for managing disruptive behaviour

www.openup.co.uk

CONTINUING PROFESSIONAL DEVELOPMENT IN THE LIFELONG LEARNING SECTOR

Peter Scales et al

9780335238170 (Paperback)
2011

eBook also available

This comprehensive guide to continuing professional development (CPD) in the lifelong learning sector (LLS) provides teachers with practical support and guidance alongside development activities. It encourages teachers to reflect on their practice and subsequently shape and develop their teaching in response to the needs of their learners, their institution and local and national priorities.

Key features:

- Provides practical and accessible guidance and information to support CPD
- Provides overviews of the main areas of teaching and learning CPD and subject-specific CPD
- Meets the needs of new teachers, trainers and tutors in the sector

www.openup.co.uk

OPEN UNIVERSITY PRESS
McGraw - Hill Education

A Quest for the Post-Historical Jesus

£2